YOM TOV SHEINI KEHILCHASO

The Second Day of Yom Tov in Israel and Abroad

Rav Yerachmiel D. Fried

adapted into English by
Moshe Dombey

Targum/Feldheim

First published 1990

ISBN 0-944070-57-4

Copyright © 1990 by Yerachmiel Dovid Fried

Phototypeset at Targum Press

Published by:
Targum Press Inc.
22700 W. Eleven Mile Rd.
Southfield, Mich. 48034

in conjunction with:
Mishnas Rishonim

Distributed by:
Feldheim Publishers
200 Airport Executive Park
Spring Valley, N.Y. 10977

Distributed in Israel by:
Nof Books Ltd.
POB 23646
Jerusalem 91235

Printed in Israel

RABBI I. J. WEISS

CHIEF RABBI

OF JERUSALEM

JERUSALEM, RECHOV YESHAYAHU 20

יצחק יעקב וייס

רב ואב״ד

לכל מקהלות האשכנזים פעיה״ק ירושלם תובב״א

מחבר שו״ת מנחת יצחק

ירושלים, רחוב ישעיהו 20

בס״ד, ירושלים, עה״ק ת״ו, יום ה׳ לס׳ כי ברוך הוא ט״ו תמוז יומא דהילולא של הרה״ק בעל האוהחה״ק זיי״ע ועכי״י תשמ״ח לפ״ק.

כן בא לפני הרה״ג המופלג מו״ה ירחמיאל דוד פריד שליט״א מטובי הלומדים בישיבה דמיר בפעיה״ק, ותלמודו בידו ספר חשוב יקר אף נעים על הלכות יו״ט שני עם פרטי דיני בני חו״ל הבאים לא״י, ובני א״י היוצאים לחו״ל הנקרא בשם יו״ט שני כהלכתו.

וראיתי דברי הרבנים הגאונים מורי ההוראה של עדתנו החרדית תכב״ץ שליט״א, המה עברו על כל הספר, ומעידים שהוא ספר נחוץ מאוד, המאסף פרטי הדינים הנוגעים למעשה בדיני יו״ט שני וברוב עמל וגיעה בירר המחבר שליט״א כל פרט ופרט מגדולי הפוסקים ראשונים ואחרונים, וגם בספיקות שנתחדשו בזמנינו ע״י ריבוי הנוסעים מהכא להתם ומהתם להכא בירר הלכה ע״י גדולי ההוראה.

ומאחר אשר בכמה תקופות קמו אינשי דלא מעלי לעקור תקנת יו״ט שני, — וכבר צווחו ע״ז ככרוכיא רבנן קמאי ובתראי שאין כח ביד שום ב״ד להתיר קדושת יו״ט שני עד ביאת משיחנו גואלנו בב״א, ואף החמירו מחמת זה בכמה דינים כי היכי דלא ליתי לזלזולי ביו״ט שני, — וביותר רבה המכשלה בעניינים אלו בזמנינו מפאת קוצר דברי הפוסקים בזה, כי בזמנם מחמת מרחק וטורח הדרך לא הי׳ נוגע כ״כ למעשה, ע״כ רבה התועלת בספרא דדין הן לחכמים מורי הוראה והן להמון העם למען ידעון המעשה אשר יעשון.

ובכן דבר נחוץ ומועיל עשה הרה״ג הנ״ל שליט״א אשר בירר וליקט פרטי הלכות אלו בלשון קלה ובסדר נאה בצירוף המקורות אשר עליהם מבסס את דבריו, ולפעלא טבא אמרין יישר, חילו לאורייתא, ויהי כאשר יצא הספר לאור עולם בטח יוקירו חובבי תורה את פעולתו, וברוך יאמרו לעומתו, ונזכה לראות במהרה בהרמת קרן התורה וישראל בבנין בניין אריאל בב״א.

הכו״ח לכבוד התורה ולומדי׳

יוסף שלו' אלישיב

ירושלים

ב"ה אדר' א' הֹ/ס/כ הֹ/ן/לֹג יֵֹשׁעֵ

לכבוד ידידי האברך הנעלה
הרה"ג ר' ירחמיאל דוד פריד שליט"א
ברכה ושלו' רב.

הריני מאשר בזה קבלת ספרו החשוב "יום-טוב שני כהלכתו"
כולל דיני ומנהגי יו"ט שני של גליות בחו"ל ובא"י לאלה הבאים
מהתם להכא ומהכא להתם.

והנה הני הילכתא הם בגדר "מקרא מועט והלכות מרובות" ומרן
הב"י לא קבע להם מקום בשלחנו הטהור אלא סימן המחזיק רק ג'
סעיפים.

ובדורנו שהשיירות מצויות טובא הרי הרבה שאלות וספיקות
צפות ועולות המבקשות את פתרונם. לכן אפריון אמטי להרה"ג
המחבר שליט"א על אשר השקיע רב עמל ללקט ולאסוף מדברי
רבותינו וסידרם בסדר נכון ואף גם הוסיף מדילי' יותר בירור וליבון
במקורות ההלכה. ולזה יהיה לתועלת להמעיינים שיתעוררו על יד
ספרו למשקל ולמטרי וממילא רווחא שמעתא.

ידידו

Rabbi CHAIM P. SCHEINBERG

KIRYAT MATTERSDORF

PANIM MEIROT 2

JERUSALEM, ISRAEL

הרב חיים פנחס שיינברג

ראש ישיבת "תורה אור"

ומורה הוראה דקרית מטרסדורף

ירושלים טל.וווווו

הנה בא לפני האברך החשוב הרב ר' ירחמיאל דוד פריד ני"י אשר רחש לבו דבר טוב ללקט ולקבץ מדברי הגמרא ופוסקים וגדולי ההוראה שליט"א את הדינים המרובים הנוגעים להלכות יו"ט שני של גליות לבני א"יי הנוסעים לחו"ל ולבני חו"ל הנוסעים לא"יי. ונחוץ מאד ספר זה בדורינו כיון שהדבר נפוץ כיום שיהודים מבקרים בחו"ל ובא"יי והדינים רבים ומסובכים הם ורק בלימוד הלכות אלה יוכלו לשמור יו"ט שני אשר הפליגו רבותינו בחומרתו, כדת וכדין.

הן אמנם באשר הוא ספר פסקי דינים הנני נמנע מליתן הסכמה לכל הנכתב. אך כיון שניכר בו עמל ויגיעה רבה ע"י תכון עמו ואמינא לפעלו טבא ואיישר חילו לאורייתא להגדיל תורה ולהאדירה, ולהוסיף זכות הרבים בעוד ספרים המועילים.

הכו"ח לכבוד התורה ולומדיה פה עיה"ק ירושלים תוב"א יום כ"ז תשרי תשמ"ח

בס"ד

ז' אדר ב' תשמ"ט
פעיה"ק ת"ו

מכתב ברכה

לכבוד מע"כ האברך היקר והנעלה הרה"ג ר' ירחמיאל ד. פריד
שליט"א מח"ס "יום טוב שני כהלכתו".
שלום רב וכט"ס.

שמחתי מאד לקבל את ספרו המקיף בהל' יום טוב שני אשר
בו אסף וליקט מדברי ראשונים ואחרונים מגדולי הפוסקים אשר
דנו בענין זה, ערוך בטוב טעם ודעת דבר דבור על אופניו ליבון
השיטות בדרך ישרה ואסוקי שמעתתא להלכתה.

והנני לברכו מעומקא דלבא דיוסיף וילך מחיל אל חיל לזכות את
הרבים בחיבורים מועילים להגדיל תורה ולהאדירה מתוך בריאות
נחת ושמחה וכט"ס אמן.

כעתירת החותם לכבודה של תורה ולומדיה

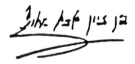

בן ציון אבא שאול

SHMUEL HALEVI WOSNER

RABBI OF

ZICHRON - MEIR, BNEI - BRAK

סמואל הלוי ואזנר

רב אב"ד ורא"ם

זברון-מאיר, בנ"י ברק

ב"ה, יום ב' פ' שמות תשמ"ח לפ"ק

הנה כבוד הרב הג' האברך המופלג בתוי"י ר' ירחמיאל דוד פריד
לאוי"ט מעיה"ק ירושלים ת"ו – זכה לחבר חיבור נאה בדיני יו"ט שני
של גליות – להבאים מהתם להכא אה"ק – ומהכא להתם. אסיפת
דינים הרבה למעשה, והוסיף גם מדיליי. ודבר טוב בעתו ובזמנו עשה
כי הלכה זו שכיחא מאד מאד בזמנינו שהולכים ובאים לזמן מועט
ומרובה ונתרבו הספיקות. וכב' המחבר אסף והעיר כיד ה' הטובה עליו
– ומכ"ש שהביא הרבה הוראות למעשה מכבוד ידידי הדגול הגאון
מהרש"ז אוערבאך שליט"א ומידידי הדגול הגאון מהרי"ש אלישיב
שליט"א – לא עברתי על כל הספר בפרטי ההלכות אבל ראיתיו ישר
הולך ובדין שיטול שכרו.

Oberrabbiner B. Stern

Taborstrasse 11 a/9
A-1020 Wien - Austria
Tel. 26 14 813

22 Sorotzkin St., Jerusalem

בצלאל בהנמוהר"א זצוק'ל שטערן
מח"ס שו"ת בצל ההכמה ב"ח
לפנים אבדק"ק הרמנשטדט. פאפא ועד"י מעלבארן יצ"ו

אבדק"ק "קהל יראים"
וינא יצ"ו

רח' סורוצקין 22. ירושלים

בס"ד

מעייכ הרה"ג חו"ב טובא מופלא ומופלג בהפלגת חכמים ירא ושלם
מאד נעלה וכו' וכו' כש"ת הר"ר ירחמיאל דוד פריעד שליט"א מסר לידי
את הכ"יי של ספרו הנחמד המכיל איסוף חשוב מאד מהלכות הנוגעות
ליו"ט שני של גליות ובמיוחד הלכות הנוגעות לדסלקא ולדנחתי זאת
אומרת לבני חו"ל העולים לא"יי לביקור ולקביעות דירה וכן לבני א"יי
הנוסעים לחו"ל לביקור ולהשתקע, שמספרם עולה בזמנינו לרבבות
רבות כ"יי ולהם שאלות ובעיות שונות איך להתנהג במקום שבאו
לשם. לזאת טרח מחברנו הי"ו ברב עמל ויגיעה לקבץ הלכות אלה
המפוזרות על פני ספרים רבים לפונדק אחד בהשכל ודעת תורה. גם
בירר וליבן הדעות שהביא בספרו בעיון מעמיק בדרך ישרה, והכל
בסדר נכון להקל על המעיין.

בודאי טוב עשה בעמו ויהי ה' אלקיו עמו להפיץ מעינותיו חוצה
לתועלת המעיינים להקל מעליהם עומס החיפוש. ועוד יזכה להמשיך
לשבת באהלה של תורה ולהוסיף אומץ כברכת ידידו חפץ בהצלחתו
ובהרמת קרנו המצפה תמיד לרחמי ה' כי לא כלו.

פעי"ק ירושלים ת"ו, י"ט בתמוז שנת תשמ"ח.

RABBI M. STERN

RABBI OF CONG. K'HAL YESODE HATORAH

FORMERLY CHIEF RABBI OF DEBRECEN

1514 — 49TH STREET

BROOKLYN, N. Y. 11219

851-5193

משה שטערן

אב״ד דעברעצין וניו־חייזל יצ״ו

בעהמ״ח שו״ת באר משה ח״ח

בלאאמו״ר הרא״ש, בעמ״ח ספרי נפי אם ומליצי אם ונש״ס

ברוקלין יע״א

בעזה״י

ראיתי הקונטרסים מלאים הלכות ברורות על כל גדותיהם בעניני
בני א״יי בחו״ל ובני חו״ל בא״יי ויסודותם בהררי קודש עם מקורות
מש״ס ופוסקים ראשונים ואחרונים שהגיש לפני הרה״ג המופלא
ומופלג בהפלגת חכמים ונבונים ירא וחרד לדבר ה׳ מו״ה ירחמיאל
פריעד מארצינו הקדושה ירושלים עיה״ק תובב״א ועברתי עליהם לפי
מיסת פנאי ומצאתי דבריו מתוקנים ונכונים ורשות ניתן לו להעתיק
מספרי באר משה על עניני בני א״יי וחו״ל מה שהוצרך לו לספרו ויה״ר
שיתקדש שם שמים ע״יי ומעומקא דלבאי מאוה לו שעוד יעלה מעלה
אחר מעלה על במתי ההצלחה ואושר האמיתי ולהוציא עוד קונטרסים
בהלכה ולמעשה ולאילנא רברבא יתעבד, צלח ורכב על דבר אמת.

RABBI B. RAKOW

RAV OF GATESHEAD

138 WHITEHALL ROAD,
GATESHEAD   NE8   1TP
Tyne & Wear
TEL. 0632-773012

בצלאל בהרה"ג ר' יום טוב ליסמאן ראקאוו

אב"ד דגייטסהעד

ב"ה יום א' פרשת פנחס תשמ"ח לפ"ק

הנה האברך המצויין וגדול בתורה הרה"ג ר' ירחמיאל דוד פריד
שליט"א שלח אלי כמה קונטרסים מספרו העומד להוציא לאור עולם
בשם ספר יו"ט שני כהלכתו שבו אסף מספרים ובירר וליבן הלכות
אלו על כל פרטיה כפי מה שראיתי ברשימה של תוכן העניינים והנה
המעט שראיתי ועיינתי מעיד על כולו שהרב הנ"ל השקיע הרבה עמל
ויגיעה על כל פרט ופרט לברר הדברים ולירד לעומקן של העניינים וגם
קיבל הוראות למעשה מגדולי א"יי שליט"א, ובכל דין ודין שכתב ציין
והראה מקור הדברים אשר אפשר לעמוד עליהם. וכבר קיבל הסכמות
מגדולי הוראה בא"יי.

הספר הנ"ל הוא דבר הנחוץ מאד ולתועלת הרבים יחשב כי לע"ע
רבו הנוסעים מהכא להתם ומהתם להכא ורבו השואלים ודבר בעתו
מה טוב.

ולזה גם ידי תיכון עמו ושיברך על המוגמר להוציא לאור את
ספרו הנ"ל לזכות את הרבים ואיישר חילו לאורייתא להגדיל תורה
ולהאדירה.

הכו"ח לכ' התורה ועומליה ולכ' המחבר שליט"א

משה הלברשטאם

מו"ץ בהערה החרדית

ראש ישיבת "דברי חיים" ססאקאוהץ

פעיה"ק י ר ו ש ל י ם תובב"א

רחוב יואל 8

בס"ד,

דבר טוב נאה ומתקבל הגה ידידנו הנכבד גברא רבא ויקירא הרה"ג
ירא וחרד לדבר ד' ותורתו מוכתר בנימוסין כש"ת מוהר"ר ירחמיאל
פריד שליט"א ממופלגי ושוקדי התורה בפעיקו"ת ירושתי"ו. אשר זה
שנים מרובות הוא משומעי לקחי ומבאי ביתי, אשר נתן לבו להעלות
על הכתב בירורים וביאורים ופסקי הלכות בענין יו"ט שני של גלויות,
דין בן חו"ל הבא לארהה"ק או בן אר"יי הנמצא בחו"ל ודעתו לחזור
וכו' כללותיהן ופרטותיהן כי רבו כמו רבו החילוקי דינים בזה. ורבים
וכן טובים נפשם בשאלתם בדבר ד' זו הלכה ברורה בדינים אלו. וזאת
מחמת שבזמן הזה התרבו מאד הנסיעות מהתם להכא ולהיפך. והואיל
ומקלעי אורחים מתרבים השאלות והספיקות וכו' ואשר על כן התעורר
המחבר הרה"ג שליט"א בעמל ויגיעה גדולה, ולחפש ולבדוק במקורות
ובחורין וסדקים בדינים אלו. וידעתי נאמנה שבכבוד ראש מרובה
העמיק והרחיב היריעה בכדי להוציא מתח"יי דבר מתוקן, ומפי סופרים
וספרים. ובעיקר שגדולי וגאוני אר"יץ שליט"א ד' יאריך ימיהם, נהגו
בו טובת עין ופשטו הרבה מספיקותיו אשר שטח לפניהם, וכמ"פ הי' לו
אתי עמי מו"מ כדרכה של תורה בהלכות אלו ומצאתי את לבבו נאמן
לדבר הלכה. וכדאי והגון וראוי להעלותו על הדפוס. ודורשי דת ודין
יביאו ברכה זו לתוך ביתם. וגם יש בזה משום זיכוי הרבים לדעת
את המעשה אשר יעשון בימים טובים לישראל, בארצה"ק תי"ו ובכל
מקומות שהם. ומגלגלין זכות על ידו. ויעזרהו השי"ת בהצלחה וסיעתא
דשמיא, אמן כיי"ר.

לרגלם התור ימי ד' לשבר שתתי תלתדתת שובעי המאי
ומלרם. שלם לתבנה דרו שת הדברים לפל.

פיעת שלום,

[חתימה]

מכתב ברכה מאת מורי ורבי הגאון שליט"א

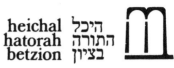

heichal
hatorah
betzion
היכל
התורה
בציון

osh Yeshiva: Rabbi Zvi Kushelevsky   ראש הישיבה: הרב צבי קושלבסקי

ס"ד מוש"ק פ' פנחס תשמ"ח

בא לפנינו ההי"ג ר' ירחמיאל פריד שליט"א וספרו בידו, ספר יו"ט
שני כהלכתו, חבור על הלכות יו"ט שני. שמחה גדולה בשבילנו לראות
בפרי בכורים של האי אילנא אשר נשתל בחצרות בית מדרשנו. כבר
לפני כמה שנים חזינו בגודל עמלו ובשקידתו היוצאת מן הכלל בחפשו
בכל כחו אחר דרך האמת בלמוד התורה, ובמאמציו הרבים לצלול
לעומק הסוגיא. ואין פלא שהצליח להוציא ספר חשוב כזה מתחת ידו,
בבחינת יגעת ומצאת תאמין.

מקובל אצלנו האימרה, דכל סברא שא"א להתיר אשת איש על פי
אל תאמר. ובבית מדרשינו הוחדר תחושה זו של אחריות באמירת
סברא לתודעה של הלומדים, ומובן מאליו שמי שלומד כך נקל לפניו
ללמוד הלכה למעשה כי כמעט שאין הבדל בין שני סוגי הילמוד,
דהיינו למוד הגמרא בעיון עד שמגיעים לאסוקי שמעתתא אליבא
דהלכתא לבין למוד הלכה למעשה לעומק עד שמגיעים לידיעת ההלכה
על בוריה.

והנה שתי דרכים לפני זה שרוצה לברר ענינים הסתומים בהלכה:
או בדרך של לקוטי ידיעות מתוך דברי התשובות של גדולי הפוסקים
ראשונים ואחרונים, או להתחקות אחרי שורשי הסוגיא בכל מקום
בש"ס שנוגע לאותה הלכה, ובדברי הראשונים ואחרונים במקום, והפוך
הפוך בה דכולה בה. והמחבר הלך בשתי דרכים ומזה ומזה לא הניח
ידו. עשה עבודה מצויינת באסיפת כל הפוסקים המדברים בענין יו"ט
שני וגם דלה דלה מבורות העמוקים של פוסקי זמננו. אבל יתרה מזה
גם השקיע עצמו בברור הסוגיא משרשיו ולן בעומקה של הלכה. והעיד
לפני שכמה פעמים התחיל כבר בסדור הספר להלכה שעדיין לא
ברור לו הגדרים של ההלכה, ולכן עזב סדור הספר וחזר לבירור הסוגיא
מראשיתו ועד סופו עוד הפעם. וזה הדבר שמקנה לו יתרון על בני גילו
המלקטים, ויעיד עליו החלק מספרו שעוסק בבירור הענינים של יו"ט
שני בעמקות והסברת הענינים בסברה ישרה. וכבר אמר החפץ חיים

יכולתי לחבר המשנה ברורה מבלי הבאור הלכה אבל יש ענין שהעולם
יראו שהמחבר יודע ספר ואפשר לסמוך עליו.

ואת זה נוכל להעיד על המחבר שבזכות עמלו ויגיעתו זכה לסייעתא
דשמיא להוציא לאור ספר חשוב. ויהא רעוא מן שמיא שיעזר להמשיך
במפעליו בהרבצת תורה לרבים, ויפוצו מעיינותיו החוצה.

CONTENTS

PREFACE

WITH IMMENSE JOY and bountiful praise to the Almighty, I present this volume to the English-speaking public. In the two short years since the publication of *Yom Tov Sheini KeHilchaso* in Hebrew, it has been accepted worldwide. In the words of HaGaon Rav Shlomo Zalman Auerbach, *shlita*, it has "filled a void in halachic literature on this subject for the rav and the layman alike."

In previous generations, international travel was a rarity; hence the relative lack of early halachic literature on this subject. But with the advent of safe, low-cost air transportation, travel between Eretz Yisrael and Chutz LaAretz became a daily occurrence, with scores of travelers journeying to and fro each year. Almost overnight, myriad questions sprang up concerning the second day of Yom Tov—questions absent from the classic halachic literature. These inquiries created the need for *Yom Tov Sheini KeHilchaso*. This translation was produced in response to many requests to make these halachos available in the vernacular.

This work was prepared under the close guidance of *gedolei Yisrael*, both Ashkenazic and Sephardic. Significant differences in Ashkenazic and Sephardic practices have been duly noted. All halachic decisions cited in the names of HaGaonim Rav Shlomo Zalman Auerbach, Rav Yosef Shalom Eliashiv, Rav Shmuel HaLevi Wosner, and Rav Ben Tziyon Abba Shaul were formulated in accordance with their directions, and reviewed by them personally.

*

First and foremost, I wish to thank the venerable and esteemed sage of Israel, Maran HaGaon Rav Shlomo Zalman Auerbach, *shlita*, who greatly encouraged me in this endeavor, often emphasizing the vital importance of a practical guide to these halachos in our generation. As with the Hebrew edition, he readily made available his precious time to discuss every nuance of this adaptation. May God grant him and all the above-mentioned *rabbonim* many more healthy years of leadership of the Jewish people.

My heartfelt gratitude also goes to the honorable HaRav Dovid Feinstein, HaRav Elimelech Bluth, and HaRav Shmuel Feurst for their invaluable aid in relating the unpublished decisions of Maran HaGaon Rav Moshe Feinstein, *zt"l*, and for clarifying those already in print.

*

In addition, I acknowledge Kollel Yismach Lev Torat Moshe of Bayit VeGan, where I presently study, and the Rosh Kollel, HaRav Pinchas Ovadiah.

*

No words can express my thanks to the Targum Press staff, particularly Rav Moshe Dombey, for his clear and lucid rendering of this work into English.

*

Finally, my dear wife, Miriam Zahava תחי', deserves the credit for this volume as well as for all my learning. May we together be privileged to see our children and our children's children involved in the study of Torah and the fear of Heaven.

*

May God reveal to us the truths of His holy Torah, lest we forbid that which is permitted or permit that which is proscribed. And may we merit the arrival of *Mashiach tzidkeinu* speedily in our days.

Yerachmiel Dovid Fried
Tammuz 5750
Yerushalayim תובב"א

INTRODUCTION

The Four Periods of Yom Tov Sheini

The Torches

When God told Moshe Rabbeinu, "This month is for you the beginning of months...,"[1] Chazal comment that He showed him the new moon and said, "When you see [the moon] in this form, sanctify it," alluding to the role of witnesses in the sanctification of each month.[2] If ever there were no witnesses, the *beis din* was to calculate when the moon should have appeared and sanctify the month on the basis of this calculation, whose formula had been handed down from generation to generation since Moshe Rabbeinu.[3]

After the *beis din* proclaimed the new month, it was to inform the people of which day was Rosh Chodesh, in order that they would celebrate the festivals at the proper time. As the Torah states, "These are the feasts of Hashem, holy convocations, which

---

1. Shemos 12:1.

2. *Sefer HaChinuch* 4; Rambam, *Mishneh Torah, Hilchos Kiddush HaChodesh* 1:3-6.

3. Ibid.

you shall proclaim in their season,"[4] and "You shall guard this statute in its appointed time...."[5]

Initially, the *beis din* sent word to those who lived far from Yerushalayim by lighting a series of torches on the mountaintops across Eretz Yisrael. But when the Kusim (Samaritans) maliciously kindled torches on the wrong nights, the *beis din* began dispatching messengers instead.[6]

The torch method remained in use from the time the Jews entered Eretz Yisrael until the days of R. Yehudah HaNassi, compiler of the Mishnah, after the destruction of the second Beis HaMikdash. During this period, there were no specific boundaries within which Yom Tov Sheini was observed. If anyone was in doubt about Rosh Chodesh—because the relay of torches did not reach his location before Yom Tov—he observed two days, no matter where he lived or what he had done in previous years. However, those Sages who calculated when Rosh Chodesh should have been were permitted to act on this calculation, even if they lived far away and did not see the torches. They did not have to fear that the witnesses had been discredited, for this was very rare.[7]

The Messengers

The route of the messengers soon determined which places would be informed of Rosh Chodesh in time to observe one day of Yom Tov, and which (those more than ten days' journey from Yerushalayim) would always observe two days. Although these areas were clearly delineated, it was only about one hundred years after R. Yehudah HaNassi that the observance of two days of Yom Tov officially became a function of location. Until then, anyone who had calculated the new moon could still observe one day, even if the messengers never reached his location before Yom Tov.[8]

---

4. Vayikra 23:4.

5. Shemos 13:10.

6. Rambam, *Hilchos Kiddush HaChodesh* 3:8.

7. *Ir HaKodesh VeHaMikdash*, vol. 3, 19:1.

8. Ibid., and 18:4.

The Second Generation of Amoraim

Only in the second generation of the Amoraim did the directive arrive from Eretz Yisrael proclaiming, "Heed the custom of your forefathers [and continue to observe two days]."[9] Henceforth, Yom Tov Sheini became a full-fledged rabbinic enactment rather than a means of resolving a doubt, and anyone living in a place unreachable by messenger had to observe two days—even a scholar.

During this period, Rabban Yochanan ben Zakai decreed that those localities reached by messenger in Nisan but not in Tishrei (when there were three fewer days to travel: the two days of Rosh HaShanah, and Yom Kippur) had to observe two days of Yom Tov all year round.[10]

The Establishment of the Calendar

The Sanhedrin continued to sanctify the months on the basis of witnesses until the end of the Talmudic period. At that time, Hillel HaNassi (son of R. Yehudah Nesia, the grandson of R. Yehudah HaNassi) foresaw that the age of *semichah* (the type of ordination dating back to Moshe Rabbeinu) was drawing to a close, and that the Sanhedrin would soon be incapable of sanctifying the months. He therefore sanctified all future months based on the calculations that form the backbone of today's Jewish calendar.

This calendar was established in 4118, 120 years after the death of the Amora Rava.[11] As a result, Jews all over the world are no longer in doubt as to when to celebrate the Jewish holidays— they need only refer to their calendars. Nevertheless, places that previously observed two days of Yom Tov continue to do so, heeding the custom of our forefathers.

---

9. *Beitzah* 4a.

10. See *Teshuvos Chasam Sofer, Orach Chaim*, no. 145.

11. Rambam, *Hilchos Kiddush HaChodesh* 5:3; *Ir HaKodesh VeHaMikdash*, vol. 3, 18:3.

The Significance of Yom Tov Sheini

"...my mother's children were angry with me; they made me the
keeper of the vineyards, but my own vineyard I have not kept"
[Shir HaShirim 1:6]. Why did I become the keeper of the
vineyards and observe two days of Yom Tov in exile? Because
"my own vineyard I have not kept"—because I did not observe
one day in Eretz Yisrael. I expected to be rewarded for observing two days [in exile] but I am only rewarded for one.

Talmud Yerushalmi, Eiruvin, chapter 3

When I lived in my land I observed one day of Yom Tov, as is
proper. But now that I have been exiled to Chutz LaAretz, I
observe two days and neither one is proper.

Tanna DeVei Eliyahu 30

The second day of Yom Tov is so sacred that God himself
concurred with its enactment and, in a sense, began to observe it
Himself. Indeed, the commentators[12] ask why Shavuos is called
"the time of the giving of our Torah" when, according to Rabbi
Yose, the Torah was given on the seventh of Sivan[13] (the fifty-first
day of the Omer) but Shavuos falls on the sixth (the fiftieth day).

The classic work *Asarah Maamaros*[14] offers the following explanation:

It is true that we celebrate a holy convocation fifty days after
Pesach, and it is also true that the exodus from Egypt took
place on a Thursday and the Torah was given on Shabbos—
fifty-one days later. But since the Torah was given in Chutz
LaAretz, God wished to endorse the second day of Yom Tov,
which Moshe added, in accordance with Rabbi Yose. By
celebrating this day Himself, the Almighty exhibited His
love for the words and decrees of the Sages of Israel, which
are sweeter to Him than the words of the Torah itself. Con-

---

12. *Teshuvos HaRivash*, no. 96; *Magen Avraham* 494.

13. See *Shabbos* 86a.

14. Cited in *Magen Avraham* 494. Also see *Teshuvos Chasam Sofer, Orach Chaim,*
no. 145.

sequently, the Torah never states that Shavuos is the day on which the Torah was given....

Clearly, the same concept underlies both Yom Tov Sheini and Moshe's adding an extra day to the three days of preparation preceding the giving of the Torah. When the Jewish people was still in the desert, prior to entering Eretz Yisrael, God concurred with Moshe's addition, thereby foreshadowing the enactment of Yom Tov Sheini in exile. By giving the Torah on the day Moshe had chosen, God alluded to the Sages' authority to sanctify a weekday. Yet the day on which He originally intended to give the Torah remains holy forever.

It is no coincidence that God chose to impart this idea through the giving of the Torah itself, for the Torah was given "in accordance with the decisions of the Sages."[15] They are empowered to interpret and determine its laws, and their rulings are incorporated into the Torah, rendering the mundane holy.

But there is a greater lesson to be learned here: although the enactments of the Sages seem no more than responses to specific situations, they actually have much deeper meanings. As the Zohar states concerning the two days of Rosh HaShanah:[16]

> "...and the judgment of His people Israel *each and every day*" [I Melachim 8:59]. What does this refer to? The two days of Rosh HaShanah. Why are there two days? In order that the two Heavenly tribunals—the strict and the merciful— should become one.

The first day is a day of strict judgment for the pure and righteous. The second day is a day of mercy for the rest of the Jewish nation. Thus, although Chazal enacted two days of Rosh HaShanah because of the doubt as to which day was actually Yom Tov,[17] with their tremendous insight into the mysteries of the Torah,

---

15. Ramban, Devarim 17:1. Also see *Pachad Yitzchak*, Shavuos 15:10.

16. Cited in *Michtav MeEliyahu*, vol. 2, p. 75.

17. *Rosh HaShanah* 30b.

they understood that both days were necessary for us to be found meritorious in judgment. The esoteric dimension of the Torah reveals the profundities behind many other "simple" rabbinic decrees.

Furthermore, it is well known that when we observe Yom Tov, we are not merely commemorating a historical event. We are basking in the same spiritual light that God revealed during the first observance of that Yom Tov.

This light shines brightest in Eretz Yisrael, "A land that Hashem, your God, cares for; the eyes of Hashem, your God, are always upon it, from the beginning of the year to the end of the year."[18] For in Eretz Yisrael the Divine Presence is manifest.[19] But in Chutz LaAretz, God's light is dimmed. Indeed, our Sages point out that one who lives in Chutz LaAretz is as if he has no God,[20] for the sanctity and spirituality of Torah observance are incomplete there. Accordingly, in Chutz LaAretz one cannot reap the full spiritual benefit of Yom Tov in one day. As Rav Saadiah Gaon asserts:[21]

> God has commanded us to observe one day of Yom Tov in Eretz Yisrael and two in Chutz LaAretz. They are both commandments of God, even though the main reason [for observing the second day] is because of doubt.

Other Gaonic sources trace the enactment of Yom Tov Sheini to the Prophets, and Rav Saadiah Gaon even writes that Yehoshua may have received this tradition from Moshe Rabbeinu.[22] In other words, the idea that a Jew in Chutz LaAretz cannot fully appreciate Yom Tov in one day may have been conveyed to Moshe by God Himself.

HaGaon Rav Shlomo Zalman Auerbach echoes this theme in an astounding statement:[23]

---

18. Devarim 11:12.

19. Kuzari 2:14.

20. Kesubos 110b.

21. Otzar HaGaonim, Beitzah 4b.

22. See Ir HaKodesh VeHaMikdash, vol. 3, 18, for a critical analysis of this view.

23. Minchas Shlomo 19:4.

Although it is called Yom Tov Sheini, God forbid that one should consider it simply an added day of Yom Tov. The Kiddush is recited because of the custom established by the Sages, and only by reciting Kiddush on *both* nights does one fulfill the mitzvah completely.

Based on this concept, some contemporary authorities contend that even a ben Eretz Yisrael who visits Chutz LaAretz must observe both days of Yom Tov since he, too, will not reap the full spiritual benefit of the holiday in one day.[24] Although this is not our custom,[25] we do not contradict its message. For spiritual light depends not only on where one *is*, but on where he *lives*. Thus, a ben Eretz Yisrael visiting Chutz LaAretz absorbs this light as if he were still in Eretz Yisrael, whereas a ben Chutz LaAretz visiting Eretz Yisrael still needs two days to truly experience it.

We can now understand the *Yerushalmi*: Since the Jews did not seek the full spiritual benefit of Yom Tov while it was available to them in Eretz Yisrael, they were exiled to a place where it is elusive. Nevertheless, in His kindness, God authorized the Sages to mitigate this decree by enacting an additional day of Yom Tov. By observing this second day, Jews can fill their homes with the full light of the holiday. Therefore, the conclusion of the *Yerushalmi* is not bleak but uplifting: "I expected to be rewarded for observing two [mediocre] days [in exile] but I am rewarded for one [excellent one]." Likewise, says *Tanna DeVei Eliyahu*, while I lived in Eretz Yisrael, *one* day of Yom Tov was proper, i.e., in that one day I internalized the essence of the holiday. But now that I observe two days in Chutz LaAretz, neither one is proper, i.e., I cannot derive the full benefit of Yom Tov from either one, only from both.

In summation, since the second day of Yom Tov was enacted to rectify our sins and restore our spirituality, God Himself consented to give the Torah on the seventh of Sivan, thereby endorsing the enactment and imbuing Yom Tov Sheini with abundant sanctity.

---

24. *Shulchan Aruch HaRav, Mahadurah Tinyana* 1:8.

25. *Shulchan Aruch* 496:3.

The Importance of Observing Yom Tov Sheini

One of our students once settled in Eretz Yisrael. Several years later, he visited our country on business....While here, he treated Yom Tov Sheini as a weekday, despite the community's protests. He died a strange death, never to return to Eretz Yisrael.

Yam Shel Shlomo, Chullin, chap. 8, no. 53

Our Sages and teachers cannot overemphasize the importance of the second day of Yom Tov, the only custom accepted by Jews all over the world, if it is indeed a custom altogether rather than an official enactment.

Although Yom Tov Sheini is based on a doubt that once existed, it overrides the mitzvah of tefillin and can postpone a *bris milah*, one of only two positive mitzvos that carry the punishment of *kares*. Lest people belittle Yom Tov Sheini, Chazal permitted the repetition of all the *berachos* recited on the first day of Yom Tov, even though when in doubt regarding blessings, we usually omit them. Moreover, those who desecrated Yom Tov Sheini (even in private) were excommunicated, and residents of Chutz LaAretz who neglected it in Eretz Yisrael were penalized. Even b'nei Eretz Yisrael visiting Chutz LaAretz were expected to honor the local custom.[26]

Throughout history, our Torah leaders have battled attempts to do away with Yom Tov Sheini. When merchants claimed that it was costing them too much money, the author of *Yad HaLevi* and R. Yosef of Slutsk, an outstanding student of HaGaon Rav Chaim of Volozhin, proved conclusively that even if Yom Tov Sheini were but a regular custom, financial loss would be no reason to abolish it.[27] Furthermore, the Yad HaLevi argues, if Chazal waived the mitzvah of tefillin, whose reward is eternal, for the sake of Yom Tov Sheini, how can we waive Yom Tov Sheini for the sake of monetary gain?[28]

---

26. *Shabbos* 23a.

27. *Kuntres Kevod Yom Tov Sheini*, at the end of "She'eilos U'Teshuvos R. Yosef MiSlutsk."

28. *Yad HaLevi*, no. 99.

In his classic work *Meshech Chochmah*,[29] Rav Meir Simcha of Dvinsk notes:

> When the Beis HaMikdash is rebuilt (may it come to pass speedily in our days), the *beis din* in Yerushalayim will once again sanctify the new moon on the basis of witnesses. If the moon is not seen on the thirtieth day of the outgoing month, the thirty-first will be declared Rosh Chodesh, even if mathematically the thirtieth should have been. Thus, Jews in the Diaspora will once again have to observe two days of Yom Tov because of doubt. Chazal therefore decreed that even today [when there is no doubt] we should observe two days [lest people say, "Last year we kept one day, so we will continue doing so this year"]. This is similar to other decrees by Rabban Yochanan ben Zakai.

Hence the vehement words of *She'eilas Yaavetz*:

> The custom of our forefathers [to observe Yom Tov Sheini] is fully in accordance with the Torah and is even more stringent than other laws. For one who fails to put on tefillin ranks among the transgressors of Israel [yet Yom Tov Sheini overrides this mitzvah]....God forbid that we should treat this custom like any other....Even if Eliyahu himself were to eliminate it, we would not listen to him....[30]

---

29. Shemos 12:1.

30. *She'eilas Yaavetz*, vol. 1, no. 168..

CHAPTER 1
The Laws of
Yom Tov Sheini

Introduction

In the days of the Beis HaMikdash, the first day of the Hebrew month was determined by the *Beis Din HaGadol* in Yerushalayim, based on the sighting of the new moon. Messengers were then sent to the outlying cities of Eretz Yisrael to inform the inhabitants of which day—the thirtieth or thirty-first of the previous month—had been declared Rosh Chodesh, the first day of the new month.

Word did not reach the Jews of Chutz LaAretz, however, until after the fifteenth of the new month. Consequently, in Tishrei and Nisan, they did not know when to observe Sukkos and Pesach. Since no Hebrew month can be longer than thirty days or shorter than twenty-nine, Yom Tov could occur on one of two possible days—fifteen days after the thirtieth of the preceding month, or fifteen days after the thirty-first. Hence the enactment of two days of Yom Tov.

The Gemara (*Beitzah* 4b) asks why both days are still observed, since Rosh Chodesh is no longer determined by the *Beis Din Ha-Gadol*, but by the fixed Jewish calendar. It concludes: "Heed the custom of your forefathers. Perhaps the government will make a decree and [people] will come to err."

Rashi explains the Gemara's fear: if the government one day forbids Torah study, people might forget how to calculate the Jewish calendar. Consequently, they might mistakenly declare Adar (normally a thirty-day month) to have twenty-nine days, begin Pesach one day early, and eat *chametz* on what is actually the last day of Pesach.[1] Chazal therefore decreed that the practice of observing two days should continue in Chutz LaAretz.[2]

Basic Laws

1. Any act forbidden on the first day of Yom Tov is also forbidden on the second day,[3] whether it is forbidden by the Torah or by rabbinic law.[4] However, certain rabbinic prohibitions may be waived on Yom Tov Sheini under pressing circumstances, as will be explained below.

2. Although Yom Tov Sheini is observed because of a doubt that once existed, Chazal took many measures to emphasize its impor-

---

1. See *Eiruvin* 39b and *Mishnah Berurah* 497:1.

2. For a description of the boundaries of Eretz Yisrael and Chutz LaAretz as they apply to the observance of Yom Tov Sheini, see chapter 18. Also see the introduction.

3. *Shulchan Aruch* 496:1. Also see *Avnei Neizer, Orach Chaim,* no. 392. The Pri Megadim (*Mishbetzos Zahav* 652:2) adds that we even forbid actions whose impermissibility on the first day of Yom Tov is debatable. In fact, whereas the Machaneh Ephraim permits smoking on the second day of Yom Tov while forbidding it on the first day, the Kesav Sofer (*Orach Chaim,* no. 66) argues that making such a distinction degrades the sanctity of Yom Tov Sheini. See *Sdeh Chemed, Maareches HaDinim,* Yom Tov 1:3.

4. Rambam, *Mishneh Torah, Hilchos Yom Tov* 1:22. Examples of rabbinic laws that apply on Yom Tov Sheini are *muktzeh,* asking a non-Jew to perform *melachah,* and traveling outside the *techum Yom Tov.*

tance.[5] For example, they suspended the mitzvah of tefillin[6] and permitted the repetition of Kiddush and all the blessings recited on the first day of Yom Tov.[7] Moreover, they imposed excommunication on anyone who neglects Yom Tov Sheini.[8]

---

5. Baal HaMaor and Raavad (beginning of *Pesachim*, chap. 4) explain that the observance of Yom Tov Sheini is more stringent than any other custom because it was accepted by all Jewish communities. Some authorities even maintain that Yom Tov Sheini is not a custom at all, but a *takanah* (rabbinic legislation). See the introduction for a full discussion.

6. *Teshuvos HaRashba* (vol. 1, no. 61) states that wearing tefillin on Yom Tov Sheini constitutes a degradation of Yom Tov. Chazal therefore suspended this mitzvah, relying on the discretionary authority granted them by the Torah. Likewise, they suspended the mitzvos of *shofar* and *lulav* when Rosh HaShanah and Sukkos fall on Shabbos. The Rashba concludes that one who wears tefillin on Yom Tov Sheini transgresses a negative commandment, "...you shall not turn aside from that which they [Chazal] teach you..." (Devarim 17:11). The Kesav Sofer infers from the Rashba that one may not wear tefillin even if he omits the blessing over the mitzvah. As a result, tefillin are *muktzeh* on Yom Tov Sheini, as they are on Shabbos and the first day of Yom Tov.

7. *Shabbos* 23a. Also see Rambam, *Hilchos Chanukah* 3:5, and *Hasagos HaRaavad* and *Maggid Mishneh* ad loc.

In his glosses on *Shulchan Aruch* 539:11, the Vilna Gaon notes that the observance of Yom Tov Sheini supersedes the commandment not to recite a blessing in vain. Also see the Vilna Gaon's comment on *Shulchan Aruch* 649:5; *Mishnah Berurah* 662:2 and 473:1; Chasam Sofer, *Orach Chaim*, no. 15; *Yeshuos Yaacov, Orach Chaim* 393:2; *Toras Rephael*, no. 1; *Divrei Malkiel*, vol. 1, no. 32; and HaGaon Rav Shlomo Zalman Auerbach, *Minchas Shlomo*, no. 19.

8. *Pesachim* 52b; Rambam, *Hilchos Yom Tov* 1:22; *Shulchan Aruch* 496:1. The Mishnah Berurah (496:1) requires the excommunication of any Jew who asks a non-Jew to do *melachah* for him on Yom Tov Sheini. Citing the Ran, he explains that in this respect, Yom Tov Sheini is more stringent than the first day of Yom Tov, when excommunication is only imposed for transgressing a Torah prohibition. Since Yom Tov Sheini is itself a rabbinic law, *any* transgression thereof—biblical or rabbinic—negates the essence of this enactment. On the first day of Yom Tov, by contrast, one who transgresses a rabbinic law has not negated the essence of the day, so his punishment is not as severe. Also see *Minchas Chinuch* 301.

The Mishnah Berurah cites other authorities who make no distinction between the first and second days of Yom Tov. (See *Shaar HaTziyun* 496:5, where this view is attributed to the Rambam.) He concludes that the imposition of excommunication for the transgression of a rabbinic law on Yom Tov Sheini is to be left to the discretion of the local *beis din*.

Preparing for the Second Day of
Yom Tov on the First Day

3. It is forbidden to prepare for the second day of Yom Tov on the
first day—even on Rosh HaShanah, which is observed for two days
even in Eretz Yisrael. This prohibition applies to actual *melachah*—
cooking, baking, etc.[9]—as well as to activities requiring time and effort
but no *melachah*,[10] e.g., washing dishes,[11] rolling a *sefer Torah* to the
place where it is to be read on the second day,[12] bringing a *siddur* to
the synagogue (even where there is an *eiruv*),[13] placing Yom Tov
candles in candlesticks,[14] or setting up tables and benches for the

---

Mabit (vol. 3, no. 149) and *Magen Avraham* (496:7) rule that a resident of Eretz
Yisrael who publicly desecrates Yom Tov Sheini in Chutz LaAretz is not subject to
excommunication, although he has acted improperly. The Maharshal (*Yam Shel
Shlomo, Chullin*, chap. 8, no. 53) reports that one such offender subsequently died a
strange death, never to return to Eretz Yisrael.

According to *Chaim She'al* (no. 55), in 5460 the elders of Yerushalayim imposed
a severe decree on visitors from Chutz LaAretz who did not observe Yom Tov Sheini
during their stay in Eretz Yisrael. We thus see how our rabbis have esteemed Yom
Tov Sheini throughout the ages.

9. *Shulchan Aruch* 503:1.

10. *Mishnah Berurah* 503:1.

11. Washing glasses in the afternoon on the first day of Yom Tov is permitted,
however, since people usually drink during the day. This is even permitted on
Shabbos, as explained in *Shulchan Aruch* 323:6. It is only forbidden to wash glasses if
they definitely will not be used that day. See *Mishnah Berurah* 323:29; *Mishneh
Halachos*, vol. 6, no. 80.

12. *Mishnah Berurah* 667:5. *Aruch HaShulchan* (667:2) advises reading a few verses
from the Torah after it is rolled to the portion for the second day; since the Torah
has then been rolled for use on the first day, the rolling is not considered an act of
preparation.

13. Thus, when Purim occurs on Saturday night, *Shaarei Teshuvah* (693:5) permits
one to bring a *Megillas Esther* to the synagogue on Shabbos—in an unobtrusive
way—only if he reads a few verses from it on Shabbos. Of course, this ruling only
applies where there is an *eiruv*, which allows one to carry on Shabbos.

14. *Mishnah Berurah* 514:35. Even after nightfall, one may only *place* the candles in
the candlesticks, not melt them in. See *Mishnah Berurah* 514:18.

next day.[15] Even when performing an action necessary for both days, one should not say it is being done for the second day.[16]

One should therefore wait until nightfall[17] before preparing for the second day of Yom Tov. Whatever cannot be prepared on the second day itself should be prepared on *erev Yom Tov*.

It is permissible to discuss plans for Yom Tov Sheini on the first day of Yom Tov.[18]

4. When food is cooked on the first day of Yom Tov, extra food for the second day may be added to the pot, provided that this addition does not entail significant time or effort.[19] Once the pot has been placed on the fire, however, food for the second day may not be added, as this would constitute a separate act—cooking for the second day.[20] Yet if extra food would enhance the flavor of the dish—for instance, adding more meat or vegetables to a stew—it may even be added after the pot has been placed on the fire.[21]

---

15. On Shemini Atzeres, the Rema (*Orach Chaim* 667) forbids arranging chairs and benches in the synagogue for Simchas Torah. However, the Mishnah Berurah (667:6) permits it at home for neatness's sake.

16. *Shulchan Aruch* 416:2. The Mishnah Berurah (290:4) notes that one who is taking a Shabbos afternoon nap should not say he is going to sleep in order to stay up late on *motza'ei Shabbos*. Also see *Mishnah Berurah* 503:6, 15.

17. *Bei'ur Halachah* (503) notes that the Pri Megadim forbids preparing for the second day of Yom Tov during twilight (*bein hashemashos*). Also see *Sho'eil U'Meishiv, Mahadurah Tinyana*, vol. 2, no. 10.

18. *Rema, Orach Chaim* 495:4, and *Mishnah Berurah* ad loc.

19. *Shulchan Aruch* 503:1. One should not explicitly state that the extra food is being added for the next day. See note 16.

The Mishnah Berurah (503:7) discusses a case where a person intends to cook for the next day, but tastes the food to circumvent the prohibition of preparing. After citing different views, he concludes that although it is preferable to act stringently, one may be lenient, provided that he cooks in the morning before the Yom Tov meal. After the meal, however, all authorities forbid cooking for the second day, even if a small amount is eaten on the first day. See *Shulchan Aruch* 503:1.

20. Rema, *Orach Chaim* 503:2; *Mishnah Berurah* 503:8.

21. *Mishnah Berurah* 503:5. Since the meat or vegetables add flavor, the extra cooking is considered necessary for the first day.

5. Under pressing circumstances, one may prepare on the first day of Yom Tov for the second day,[22] provided that no actual *melachah*—such as cooking or baking—is performed.[23] This should be done as early in the day as possible, with some change (*shinui*) in the normal manner of preparation.[24]

Preparing for the Second Day of Yom Tov on Chol HaMoed

6. During Chol HaMoed, one may prepare for the second day of Yom Tov[25] by purchasing food and drink, cooking, and performing any *melachos* involving the preparation of food.[26]

---

22. On the first day of Yom Tov, the Mishnah Berurah (667:5) permits one to bring wine or water to wherever he'll be eating the next day if this would be difficult to do that night.

23. This is clearly indicated by *Chayei Adam* 153:6.

24. *Mishnah Berurah* (667:5) explains that the wine or water should be brought as early in the day as possible so it will not be apparent that it is being brought for the next day. Also see *Shaar HaTziyun* 503:2.

25. Although it is forbidden to prepare for after a holiday on Chol HaMoed, the Tur takes note of the dispute over whether this prohibition applies to preparing for Yom Tov Sheini, which is actually a weekday according to the Torah. He reports that the Rosh rules leniently in this matter, as does the Rema (*Orach Chaim* 539:11). Also see *Divrei Yisrael* (Weltz), *Orach Chaim*, no. 141, and *Levushei Mordechai, Mahadurah Tlisai*, no. 48.

26. R. Akiva Eiger infers from the Tur that one may perform *melachah* on Chol HaMoed for Yom Tov Sheini. His view is cited by the Mishnah Berurah (539:39).

The Pri Megadim (*Eshel Avraham* 539:11) disagrees, and *Hissorerus Teshuvah* (vol. 1, no. 98) points out that the Rema explicitly permits only purchasing, which implies that he forbids actual *melachah*.

Nevertheless, HaGaon Rav Shlomo Zalman Auerbach accepts the view of R. Akiva Eiger and the Mishnah Berurah. In *Minchas Shlomo* (no. 19), HaGaon Rav Auerbach compares their position to the permission given to recite Kiddush and refrain from wearing tefillin on Yom Tov Sheini in order to impress upon people the seriousness of the day. *Eshel Avraham* (Butchach) (530) adds that even those authorities who view *melachah* on Chol HaMoed as contrary to a Torah prohibition explain that the Torah left it to Chazal to determine the nature and extent of this prohibition. It was therefore within their authority to exclude preparation for Yom Tov Sheini from the proscription.

Eating a Meal on *Erev Yom Tov Sheini*

7.   In the final three "hours"[27] of the first day of Yom Tov, it is a mitzvah[28] to refrain from beginning a meal, lest one spoil his appetite for the evening meal of Yom Tov Sheini.[29]

If Yom Tov falls on Shabbos and Sunday, the third Shabbos meal should begin before the end of the ninth "hour."[30] One may even begin after this time, but only a small amount of bread should be eaten.[31]

Eiruv Tavshilin

8.   If the second day of Yom Tov occurs on Friday, one may only cook and prepare for Shabbos on that day if an *eiruv tavshilin* was

---

Hissorerus Teshuvah distinguishes between food preparation and other *melachos* performed in honor of Yom Tov Sheini. R. Akiva Eiger states only that *cooking* is permitted, possibly implying that other types of *melachah* are forbidden. This matter remains unclear, and a halachic authority should be consulted. Also see *Divrei Yisrael, Orach Chaim*, no. 141.

27.   *Shulchan Aruch* 249:2 and *Mishnah Berurah* 249:17. An "hour" is calculated by dividing the time between sunrise and sunset by twelve. Thus, "the final three 'hours' " refers to the last quarter of the day.

28.   Rema, *Orach Chaim* 529:1. The Mishnah Berurah (529:5) notes that it is not *forbidden* to eat a meal late in the day—it is merely a mitzvah not to, even if one desires only a small meal (see *Mishnah Berurah* 249:15). By contrast, it is prohibited to begin a large meal late in the afternoon before Shabbos or Yom Tov. See *Shulchan Aruch* 249:2. Also see *Hissorerus Teshuvah*, vol. 2, no. 53.

29.   Although the Rema cited in note 28 refers specifically to beginning a meal late in the day prior to the first day of Yom Tov, the Magen Avraham extends this ruling to the eve of Yom Tov Sheini. The Bei'ur Halachah (529, s.v. "MiMinchah") questions the logic of the Magen Avraham but notes that many later authorities concur with him. Also see *Kesav Sofer, Orach Chaim*, no. 118, and *Hissorerus Teshuvah*, vol. 2, no. 53.

30.   *Mishnah Berurah* 529:8.

31.   *Shaar HaTziyun* (529:10), citing *Machatzis HaShekel*, rules that one should eat at least a *kebeitzah* (the volume of an egg) of bread, the amount needed to fulfill the mitzvah of eating a Shabbos meal. One may eat more than this, but less than he is accustomed to eat during the week.

prepared before Yom Tov.[32] Even if an *eiruv tavshilin* was prepared, however, it is forbidden to cook on Thursday, the first day of Yom Tov, for Shabbos.[33] (See chapter 3, paragraphs 4-6, for further details.)

Candlelighting on the Second Night of Yom Tov

9. Candles are lit on the second night of Yom Tov, and the

---

32. *Mishnah Berurah* 527:1. The mitzvah of *eiruv tavshilin* is fulfilled by setting aside two cooked foods before Yom Tov and reciting the blessing "*al mitzvas eiruv*," followed by these words: "Through this *eiruv*, may it be permitted for us to bake, cook, keep food warm, kindle lights, and do anything on Yom Tov in preparation for Shabbos, for us and all who live in this city." The *eiruv* is then eaten on Shabbos, customarily at the third Shabbos meal.

The *Shulchan Aruch* (527:22) rules that if one remembers on Thursday, the first day of Yom Tov, that he did not set aside an *eiruv tavshilin*, he may do so on Thursday, reciting the following condition: "If today is actually Yom Tov, no *eiruv* is necessary [since the second day will not be Yom Tov]. If tomorrow is Yom Tov, through this *eiruv* may it be permitted for us...." No blessing should be recited in this situation. See *Mishnah Berurah* 527:74 and *Shaar HaTziyun* 527:94. A conditional *eiruv* may also be prepared on the first day of Rosh HaShanah for the second day.

One who forgets to set aside an *eiruv* may rely on the *eiruv* prepared by the rav or rabbinical court of the city on behalf of the local residents. However, the *Shulchan Aruch* (527:7) and *Mishnah Berurah* (ad loc.) explain that the community *eiruv* may only be used by someone who fails to make an *eiruv* due to pressing circumstances, someone whose *eiruv* was lost before his Shabbos preparations were complete, or someone who does not know how to make an *eiruv*. A person who fails to make an *eiruv* due to laziness or willful neglect may not rely on the community's *eiruv*. The Mishnah Berurah adds that a person who forgets twice in a row to make an *eiruv* is considered guilty of "willful neglect."

33. *Shulchan Aruch* 527:13 and *Mishnah Berurah* ad loc. When Yom Tov Sheini falls on Shabbos, many authorities rule that, when cooking for Shabbos, the food should be prepared far enough in advance that there would still be time to eat it before Shabbos. In this way, at least theoretically, the cooking can be considered to have been done for the first day of Yom Tov. The Mishnah Berurah (527:3) states that this view should also be taken into account when Yom Tov Sheini falls on Friday, even though cooking on the second day of Yom Tov is prohibited only by rabbinic decree. But if necessary, one may rely on the lenient view. If the first day of Yom Tov falls on Friday, however, the lenient view should only be relied on where there is a dire need.

blessing *"lehadlik ner shel Yom Tov"* is recited.[34] If the second night of Yom Tov occurs on Shabbos, the blessing *"lehadlik ner shel Shabbos veshel Yom Tov"* is recited.[35]

10. A woman who is accustomed to recite the *shehecheyanu* blessing when she lights candles[36] on the first night of Yom Tov should do so on the second night as well.[37] The only Yamim Tovim on which *shehecheyanu* is not recited are the last two days of Pesach.[38]

On the second night of Rosh HaShanah, a woman who recites *shehecheyanu* should wear a new garment and intend that the blessing include the garment as well as the holiday.[39] If she does not have a new

---

34. The Gemara does not state that it is a mitzvah to light candles for Yom Tov. *Hagahos Maimoni (Hilchos Shabbos 5:1)* and *Or Zarua (Hilchos Shabbos, no. 11)* cite the Talmud Yerushalmi as the source for this mitzvah. In any case, the *Shulchan Aruch* (263:5 and 514:11) rules that the blessing is recited and the Mishnah Berurah (514:48) extends this ruling to Yom Tov Sheini as well.

HaGaon Rav Ovadia Yossef (*Yechaveh Daas*, vol. 1, no. 27) reports that Yemenite Jews customarily omit the blessing, since Rambam only mentions it when discussing Shabbos. But he advises Yemenite women in Eretz Yisrael to adopt the local custom and recite the blessing. See *Halichos Bas Yisrael* (English edition), chap. 17, note 12. Also see *Har Tzvi, Orach Chaim*, no. 141, as to whether one fulfills the mitzvah with a candle that was lit on the first night and continues to burn on the second night.

35. *Mishnah Berurah* 263:24.

36. In his commentary on *Shulchan Aruch* 263:5, R. Akiva Eiger notes that *She'eilas Yaavetz* could not find a source for this custom. The Mishnah Berurah (263:23) nevertheless concludes that one need not object to it. See *Halichos Bas Yisrael* (English edition), chap. 17, par. 13, with its notes, for a full discussion.

37. All blessings recited on the first day of Yom Tov are repeated on the second day.

38. The last two days of Pesach are not a new holiday; thus, *shehecheyanu* is not recited, even on the first night. See *Shulchan Aruch* 490 and *Mishnah Berurah* ad loc.

39. *Mishnah Berurah* 600:4; *Mateh Ephraim* 599:9. The need for either a new garment or a new fruit for *shehecheyanu* on the second night of Rosh HaShanah is based on the halachic principle of *kedushah achas* (one sanctity), which means that the two days of Rosh HaShanah are halachically considered one day (see chapter 2, note 17). This concept leads some authorities to conclude that *shehecheyanu* should be omitted on the second night of the holiday. However, most authorities consider Rosh HaShanah no different from other Yamim Tovim, on which *shehecheyanu* is recited both nights. To accommodate the divergent views, it is customary to wear a new garment or eat a new fruit, with the intention that one's *shehecheyanu* apply to the garment or the fruit as well as the holiday.

garment, she should place a new fruit on the table, bearing it in mind when she recites the blessing. In this case, she should light the candles just before Kiddush.[40] If she has neither a new garment nor a new fruit, she may recite *shehecheyanu* without them.[41]

11. Some authorities rule that candles should not be lit on the second night of Yom Tov until nightfall.[42] Others permit lighting late in the afternoon if the room has become dim.[43]

---

40. *Mateh Ephraim* 599:9. This is done to minimize the interruption between saying *shehecheyanu* and eating the new fruit. The recitation of Kiddush is not an interruption since it is forbidden to eat before Kiddush. Also see *Avnei Neizer, Orach Chaim*, no. 450. *Kaf HaChaim* (*Orach Chaim* 600:6) explains that since the majority view mandates the recitation of *shehecheyanu* on the second night (see note 39), and the fruit serves only to accommodate a minority view, we may rely on another minority view, which permits *shehecheyanu* to be recited on *seeing* a new fruit, even if it is not eaten immediately. See *Shulchan Aruch* 225:3.

41. *Shulchan Aruch* 600:2; *Mishnah Berurah* 600:5. The Mishnah Berurah explains that although the two days have "one sanctity," they are still separate and *shehecheyanu* is recited on each of them; since this is the majority view, the blessing should be recited even if no new garment or fruit is available. In fact, *Maasei Rav* (par. 210) reports that the Vilna Gaon made no effort to obtain a new fruit for the second night.

42. In the introduction to the Perishah's commentary on the *Tur, Yoreh Deah*, his son cites this ruling in the name of his mother, whom the Noda BeYehudah described as "a woman whose heart was uplifted with wisdom." Lighting candles before dark is considered "preparing" for the next day. This is also the conclusion of HaGaon Rav Shlomo Zalman Auerbach.

43. *Mishnah Berurah* 514:33. Since their light is then being used on the first day of Yom Tov, lighting the candles is not considered preparing for the next day. HaGaon Rav Shlomo Zalman Auerbach notes that the exact time one would be permitted to light the candles depends on how much sunlight is entering the room. Also see *Halichos Beisah*, chap. 14, note 108, in the name of the Levush. The Shelah advocates lighting before the men come home from shul, so those at home will not sit in the dark.

Maariv, Kiddush, and Havdalah

12. *Maariv* should not be recited until after dark on Yom Tov Sheini.[44] After *maariv,* Kiddush is recited,[45] including the *shehecheyanu* blessing.

13. When Yom Tov Sheini begins on Saturday night, "*VaTodieinu*" (the Havdalah prayer) is inserted in *Shemoneh Esrei.*[46] The order of Kiddush and Havdalah follows the acronym YaKNeHaZ: *Yayin, Kiddush, Ner, Havdalah, Zeman* (the blessings over wine, Kiddush, fire, Havdalah, and time [*shehecheyanu*]).[47]

The Havdalah blessing concludes with the words "*Hamavdil*

---

44. Reciting *maariv* before dark would degrade the first day of Yom Tov. The Levush (*Orach Chaim* 488) adds that if we recite *maariv* before dark, people might think it permissible to prepare for the next day before dark as well. Also see *Kaf HaChaim, Orach Chaim* 639:57.

Rav Pe'alim (vol. 4, no. 23) does permit one to light candles and recite Kiddush before dark on Yom Tov Sheini in cases of great need. In *Moriah* (Shevat 5749), HaGaon Rav Yitzchak Yaacov Weiss applied this ruling to reciting Kiddush for hospital patients on the last night of Pesach and the second night of Shavuos (but not on Sukkos, for reasons discussed there). On the second night of Pesach, Kiddush may not be recited before dark because of the requirement to drink four cups of wine at the Seder. Similarly, on the first night of Shavuos, Kiddush may not be recited before dark, for there must be forty-nine complete days—seven full weeks—of *sefiras ha'omer.*

Also see *Shemiras Shabbos KeHilchasah,* vol. 2, chap. 47, note 111, where the ruling of HaGaon Rav Shlomo Zalman Auerbach is cited: One may recite Kiddush for an elderly or sick person before dark even when Yom Tov falls on Saturday night. Of course, one may not recite the blessing over fire—or perform any *melachah*—until after dark.

45. *Shulchan Aruch* 473:1 and 662:2. Also see paragraph 2 and note 7.

46. "*VaTodieinu*" marks the transition from the sanctity of Shabbos to the sanctity of Yom Tov. Havdalah is not recited over the transition from the first day of Yom Tov to the second, even though the sanctity of the first day is greater than that of the second.

47. Some people are accustomed to wear a new garment or eat a new fruit on the second night of Yom Tov (see notes 39-41 concerning the second night of Rosh HaShanah), but the Mishnah Berurah (600:5) disapproves. See *Birkei Yosef* 621:25, which attempts to justify this practice.

bein kodesh lekodesh" (who separates one kind of sanctity [Shabbos] from another[48] [Yom Tov]).[49] The blessing over spices is omitted.[50]

14. Some authorities rule that the flames of the two Yom Tov candles should not be joined for the blessing over fire, as is customary during the rest of the year. Rather, the two candles should be brought as close together as possible without their flames or the candles themselves touching; if the flames do join, they may be separated.[51] Others state

---

48. *Shulchan Aruch* 473:1. The Rashbam (commenting on *Pesachim* 103a) explains that we recite Havdalah, which formally ends Shabbos, after Kiddush, which formally begins Yom Tov, lest Shabbos appear to be a burden.

49. One who wishes to perform a type of *melachah* permitted on Yom Tov before Kiddush on Saturday night should either say *"Baruch hamavdil bein kodesh lekodesh"* or recite *maariv*, inserting *"VaTodieinu"* in *Shemoneh Esrei*. See *Magen Avraham* 199:13 and *Eshel Avraham* ad loc.

50. *Mishnah Berurah* 473:3.

51. The Mordechai (*Pesachim* 103b) cites the interpretation of the Ri of Kurbiel: although it is preferable to light an *avukah* (a double-wick candle) for Havdalah, if one single-wick candle has already been lit, there is no need to light another. The Magen Avraham (298:4) requires an *avukah*, however, and insists that the two wicks be connected. R. Akiva Eiger, in his glosses on *Magen Avraham*, argues that there is no need to connect the wicks in order to fulfill the requirement of *avukah*.

Although it is customary to follow the Magen Avraham and use a double-wick candle for Havdalah, HaGaon Rav Shlomo Zalman Auerbach advises against combining the two Yom Tov candles to form an *avukah*, lest the dripping of the wax reduce their burning time, which is tantamount to extinguishing them according to some authorities. *VaYaged Moshe* (15:9) cites *Minhagei Chabad*, which reports that in the home of Rav Shneur Zalman of Liadi the Yom Tov candles were not combined. Likewise, when the blessing was recited, the participants would gaze at the candles without holding their fingernails up to the light, as is customary throughout the year.

Another problem is raised by Rav Tzvi Cohen in *Erev Pesach SheChal BeShabbos*: Separating the candles may be considered extinguishing them (see *Mishnah Berurah* 502:19). He advises lighting two matches from the Yom Tov candles, reciting the blessing over them, and putting them down while they are still connected, allowing them to burn out by themselves.

However, HaGaon Rav Yosef Shalom Eliashiv stresses that fire may be kindled on Yom Tov only for the sake of Yom Tov, and that authorities debate whether this mitzvah is performed for the sake of Yom Tov. HaGaon Rav Eliashiv therefore prefers the option cited in his name in note 53.

that the flames[52] should be connected,[53] but not the candles.

Medicine

15.   Any *melachah* forbidden by Torah law on Shabbos may not be performed on Yom Tov Sheini for a sick person unless his life is in danger.[54] If his life is not in danger but his illness affects his whole body, a non-Jew may be asked to perform any *melachah* necessary for his recovery.[55]

16.   Any act forbidden by rabbinic law on Shabbos may be performed on Yom Tov Sheini for a sick person, even if his life is not in danger[56]

---

52. *Yesod VeShoresh HaAvodah, Shaar Teshi'i,* cited in *Elef HaMagen* on *Mateh Ephraim* 600:3. This view is accepted by HaGaon Rav Yosef Shalom Eliashiv, who requires that the flames be joined.

53. This view is based on a ruling by HaGaon Rav Yosef Shalom Eliashiv. The contact of the candles may involve the *melachah* of *memacheik* (smoothing or scraping), but if there is contact, they may be separated. In an appendix to *Erev Pesach SheChal BeShabbos,* HaGaon Rav Sarya Deblitzki suggests cutting off a small part of a Havdalah candle before Shabbos and placing it in a separate candlestick. After reciting the blessing, this candle should be left burning until it goes out by itself. However, the objection raised in note 51 to the procedure suggested by Rav Tzvi Cohen would also apply to this suggestion.

54. *Shulchan Aruch* 496:2. In general, any action prohibited on Shabbos and Yom Tov by Torah law may not be performed by a Jew unless there is danger to life. This restriction applies to both days of Yom Tov.

55. *Mishnah Berurah* 496:8; *Shaar HaTziyun* 496:9-10. On Shabbos, the first day of Yom Tov, and both days of Rosh HaShanah (see chapter 2, note 17), any act prohibited by Torah law may not be performed for a sick person, even if it is done in an unusual manner (*shinui*). *Shaar HaTziyun* questions whether a *shinui* would make such an act permissible on Yom Tov Sheini.

56. *Shulchan Aruch* 496:2. On Shabbos, the first day of Yom Tov, and both days of Rosh HaShanah, one may only perform an action forbidden by rabbinic law if the illness affects the entire body.

and even if he is suffering from a localized illness,[57] like an eye infection.[58] Likewise, medicine may be taken for any kind of pain, even a localized one.[59]

Immersion in the *Mikvah*

17. A woman[60] who must immerse in the *mikvah* on the night of Yom Tov Sheini should perform her preparations before Yom Tov.[61]

Afterward she should tie her hair to prevent it from becoming tangled and, if possible, avoid handling sticky foods. If she does touch such foods, she should wash her hands immediately.[62]

---

57. Rema, *Orach Chaim* 496:2.

58. *Mishnah Berurah* 496:5. Since an eye infection does not affect the rest of the body, it is forbidden to treat it on Shabbos or Yom Tov, even with a *shinui*. But on Yom Tov Sheini, the eye may be treated even without a *shinui*. Also see *Avnei Neizer*, *Orach Chaim*, nos. 394:21-23, 395.

59. *Mishnah Berurah* 496:5. Taking medicine on Shabbos and Yom Tov is forbidden by rabbinic decree—lest a person grind medicinal herbs (*tochein*). This decree does not apply to any illness that affects the entire body. On Yom Tov Sheini, it does not apply to any illness that is causing pain.

HaGaon Rav Yosef Shalom Eliashiv rules that one may not ask a non-Jew to change the battery in his hearing aid on Yom Tov Sheini, because a hearing impairment is not considered an illness.

60. See chapter 4, paragraph 5, concerning a resident of Eretz Yisrael who spends Yom Tov in Chutz LaAretz.

61. *Shulchan Aruch, Yoreh Deah* (199:6). *Badei HaShulchan* (199:67) notes that she need not prepare just before sunset, as she normally does, since she will not immerse that night anyway. If she plans to handle sticky foods, she should prepare after finishing with them.

62. *Shulchan Aruch, Yoreh Deah* 199:6. Before immersing, she should inspect herself thoroughly and wash herself internally with warm water. She may use water heated on Yom Tov. She should also brush her teeth with a dry toothbrush so that no food particles remain in her mouth.

Bris Milah

18. A postponed *bris milah* may not be performed on Shabbos or either day of Yom Tov.[63]

19. If a baby is born during twilight, making it unclear whether Yom Tov Sheini is the eighth day after birth, some authorities favor postponing the *bris* until after Yom Tov.[64] Others permit the *bris* to be performed on Yom Tov Sheini[65] without hesita-

---

63. *Shulchan Aruch, Yoreh Deah* 266:8. The Rambam (*Hilchos Milah* 1:15) rules that a postponed *bris milah* may be performed on Yom Tov Sheini. This view, shared by many early authorities, is accepted by the Shach (266:8) and the Vilna Gaon. The Noda BeYehudah (*Mahadurah Kama, Orach Chaim*, no. 30) permits relying on this opinion, but he himself does not. HaGaon Rav Moshe Feinstein, HaGaon Rav Shlomo Zalman Auerbach, and HaGaon Rav Yosef Shalom Eliashiv also rule stringently in this matter. See *Be'er Moshe*, p. 242.

64. The halachic status of twilight is unclear: is it the end of one day or the beginning of the next? Consequently, a baby born Friday evening at twilight may not be circumcised on either Friday or Shabbos: since he may have been born on Shabbos, he may not be eight days old on Friday; since he may have been born on Friday, he may be nine days old on Shabbos, and only a *bris* performed on the eighth day may be performed on Shabbos. The baby's *bris milah* is therefore postponed until Sunday. Likewise, according to the *Shulchan Aruch* (*Yoreh Deah* 266:18), where the eighth day in question is Yom Tov Sheini, the *bris* is performed the day after Yom Tov. This is also the view of the Chasam Sofer (*Yoreh Deah*, no. 252) and *Kinyan Torah* (vol. 1, no. 99). HaRav Dovid Feinstein and HaRav Elimelech Bluth report that this was the ruling of HaGaon Rav Moshe Feinstein as well. Rav Y. A. Penfil has informed me that HaGaon Rav Moshe Stern, HaGaon Rav Moshe Bik, and HaGaon Rav Menashe Klein concur, and this is the custom in America.

65. In his glosses on the *Shulchan Aruch*, R. Akiva Eiger notes that the *av beis din* of Berlin disagreed with the *Shulchan Aruch*. In fact, the Noda BeYehudah (in *Mahadurah Kama, Orach Chaim*, no. 30, and in his glosses on the *Shulchan Aruch, Dagul Mervavah*) interprets the *Shulchan Aruch* itself to rule leniently. This is also the position of both HaGaon Rav Shlomo Zalman Auerbach and HaGaon Rav Yosef Shalom Eliashiv.

Chazal question whether a baby delivered by caesarian section may be circumcised on Shabbos. Because the Gemara fails to arrive at a definitive conclusion, the *Shulchan Aruch* (*Yoreh Deah* 266:10) rules that such a *bris* should not be performed on Shabbos or Yom Tov. Since this ruling is based on a doubt, both HaGaon Rav Shlomo Zalman Auerbach and HaGaon Rav Yosef Shalom Eliashiv argue that if a baby born during *bein hashemashos* may be circumcised on Yom Tov Sheini, so may a baby born by caesarian section. Also see *Teshuvos Chasam Sofer, Yoreh Deah*, no. 250; Rav Moshe Sternbuch, *Teshuvos VeHanhagos*, no. 594; and *Neta Gavriel*, Yom Tov 44:4. Rav Y. A. Penfil reports that HaGaon Rav Moshe Stern heard this ruling from the late Satmar Rav.

tion.[66] All authorities concur that when this situation occurs on the second day of Rosh HaShanah, the *bris* is postponed until the next day.[67]

An *Aravah* Uprooted on Yom Tov

20. An *aravah* (willow branch) that was uprooted on Yom Tov Sheini is *muktzeh* and may not be used as part of the four species, even if a non-Jew uprooted it for his own use.[68] If such a branch is bound with the other species, the entire bundle is *muktzeh*.[69]

21. A willow branch that was uprooted on the first day of Sukkos may be used on Yom Tov Sheini[70] unless the first day of Yom Tov was Shabbos.[71]

According to the above view of HaGaon Rav Moshe Feinstein, it is forbidden to perform a *bris* on Yom Tov Sheini if the baby was delivered by caesarian section. *Mohelim* in the United States follow this opinion.

66. This is the conclusion of HaGaon Rav Aharon Kotler in *Mishnas Rav Aharon* 11:3.

67. *Mateh Ephraim* 596:14 and *Mishnas Rav Aharon* 11:3. This is based on the principle of *kedushah achas*, as explained in chapter 2, note 17.

68. *Mishnah Berurah* 655:3. A willow branch uprooted on the first day of Sukkos is also *muktzeh* according to *Teshuvos HaRashba* (vol. 1, no. 297), the Magen Avraham, and the Mishnah Berurah. *Shaar HaMelech* (Hilchos Yom Tov 2:18), however, concludes that the Torah mitzvah of taking the four species on the first day of Sukkos overrides the rabbinic prohibition of *muktzeh*. Also see *Orchos Chaim* (Sphinka) 655 and *Sdeh Chemed, Kellalim* 141:4.

Concerning a resident of Chutz LaAretz who is visiting Israel and has no other willow, see chapter 3, paragraph 7.

69. See the Maharsham on *Shulchan Aruch* 655 and *Minchas Yitzchak*, vol. 8, no. 59.

70. *Mishnah Berurah* 655:3. A second day of Yom Tov is observed in the Diaspora in case the first day is not actually Yom Tov. If Yom Tov Sheini is Yom Tov, the willow was picked *erev Yom Tov* and is not *muktzeh*. On the other hand, if the first day was actually Yom Tov, the second is not, in which case the willow is certainly usable.

71. Since it was not prepared before Shabbos, the willow may not be used on Sunday; things prepared on Shabbos may not be used on Yom Tov—see *Beitzah* 2b.

Melachah Performed by a Non-Jew on the First Day of Yom Tov

22. If a non-Jew performs *melachah* for a Jew on Yom Tov,[72] it is forbidden to derive benefit from it the entire day, and any product of this *melachah* is *muktzeh*.[73] In Eretz Yisrael, where only one day of Yom Tov is observed, a Jew may not derive benefit until enough time has passed after Yom Tov for the *melachah* to have been done. This time period is known as *kedei sheyaaseh*.[74]

23. In Chutz LaAretz, authorities debate the application of *kedei sheyaaseh* when a non-Jew does *melachah* on a Jew's behalf on the

---

72. *Shulchan Aruch* 515:1-5. If the act performed by the non-Jew is forbidden (to a Jew) by Torah law, no Jew may benefit from it; if the non-Jew's act involved only a rabbinic prohibition, only the Jew for whom the work was done is forbidden to benefit from it. See *Mishnah Berurah* 515:52.

73. For example, if a non-Jew uprooted a willow branch for a Jew, the Jew may not smell it. See *Amudei Ohr*, nos. 11-17, and *Har Tzvi, Orach Chaim*, vol. 1, no. 183.

The Rema (*Orach Chaim* 515:1) adds that if a non-Jew has performed *melachah* in preparing food for a Jew, even if the Jew has already recited a blessing and put the food in his mouth, the food is *muktzeh* and must be removed.

74. There is a dispute as to whether *kedei sheyaaseh* is required only for the Jew on whose behalf the *melachah* was done, or for any Jew.

According to Rashi, *kedei sheyaaseh* is designed to prevent one from deriving any benefit—even by saving time—from work done by a non-Jew on Yom Tov. Therefore, any Jew must wait *kedei sheyaaseh* before deriving benefit from the work.

Tosafos argues that *kedei sheyaaseh* is intended to discourage a Jew from asking a non-Jew to do work for him on Yom Tov. Consequently, only the Jew who asks must wait; other Jews may derive benefit from the work immediately after Yom Tov.

Rashi and Tosafos also dispute the amount of time required by *kedei sheyaaseh*. According to Rashi, after Yom Tov one must wait only as long as it would take to actually perform the *melachah*, e.g., uprooting vegetables from the ground. According to Tosafos, however, one must wait as much time as it takes to reach the field as well; otherwise, a Jew might still be motivated to ask a non-Jew to go out to the field for him on Yom Tov. See Tosafos, *Eiruvin* 39b.

A third view, that of the Rosh, maintains that instead of waiting however long it would take to reach the field from which the non-Jew actually picked the vegetables, one may wait only as long as it would take to reach the closest field in which produce grows.

The *Shulchan Aruch* (515:1) rules in favor of Tosafos.

first day of Yom Tov. Some allow the Jew to benefit from the *melachah* after waiting *kedei sheyaaseh* at the conclusion of the first day, while others require him to wait *kedei sheyaaseh* after the second.[75] It is customary to follow the stringent view,[76] unless guests arrive and the *melachah* proves necessary for them.[77] Some authorities even allow the Jew for whom the *melachah* was done to rely on the lenient view when there is a pressing need.[78]

All opinions concur that on Rosh HaShanah one must wait *kedei sheyaaseh* following the second day of Yom Tov.[79]

Melachah Performed by a Non-Jew on Yom Tov Sheini

24. If a non-Jew performs *melachah* for a Jew on Yom Tov Sheini, the Jew must wait *kedei sheyaaseh* before deriving benefit from it.[80]

---

75. See the dispute between Rashi and Tosafos, in the preceding note, over the reason for the enactment of *kedei sheyaaseh*. According to Rashi, a Jew may derive benefit from the *melachah* of a non-Jew after the first day of Yom Tov, for if the first day was actually Yom Tov, the second day is not, and if the second day is actually Yom Tov, the non-Jew's work was done on *erev Yom Tov*. According to Tosafos, since it is forbidden to ask a non-Jew to perform *melachah* on either day, a Jew may not derive benefit on either day. Most authorities concur with Rashi, and his view is accepted in *Shulchan Aruch* (515:1).

76. Rema, *Orach Chaim* 515:1. See *Mishnah Berurah* 515:9 and *Shaar HaTziyun* 515:14. Also see note 74 regarding the time period of *kedei sheyaaseh*. Although the *Shulchan Aruch* rules in favor of Tosafos, the *Bei'ur Halachah* (s.v. "VeShiur"), concludes that if the non-Jew performed the *melachah* on the first day of Yom Tov, one may rely on the Rosh when waiting *kedei sheyaaseh* after the second day.

77. Rema, *Orach Chaim* 515. Also see *Mishnah Berurah* 515:12 and *Shaar HaTziyun* 515:16.

78. *Mishnah Berurah* (515:13) cites the Taz to this effect. *Shaar HaTziyun* (515:26), however, quotes *Chayei Adam* and *Shulchan Aruch HaRav*, which permit no such leniency. The author concludes that although one should follow *Chayei Adam*, if one is uncertain whether the *melachah* was performed on Yom Tov or *erev Yom Tov*, he may rely on Rashi.

79. *Shulchan Aruch* 515:1. This is based on the concept of *kedushah achas* (see note 39).

80. Ibid. This is in order that the second day of Yom Tov will not be taken less seriously than the first day.

25. If Yom Tov occurs on Thursday and Friday and a non-Jew performed *melachah* on behalf of a Jew on Thursday, the Jew may derive benefit from the *melachah* on Friday night, after waiting *kedei sheyaaseh*.[81] If the product of the *melachah* requires preparation forbidden on Shabbos, it remains *muktzeh* on Shabbos.[82]

When Rosh HaShanah occurs on Thursday and Friday, however, the Jew may not derive benefit from the *melachah* until the end of Shabbos.[83] Some authorities even require him to wait *kedei sheyaaseh* after Shabbos.[84]

Melachah Performed by a Jew on Yom Tov Sheini

26. If a Jew deliberately performs *melachah* on Yom Tov Sheini, others may derive benefit from it after Yom Tov[85] but he may not. If the *melachah* was performed unintentionally, both he and other Jews may derive benefit from it after Yom Tov.[86]

---

81. Rema, *Orach Chaim* 515:4.

82. Ibid.

83. Ibid.

84. *Mishnah Berurah* 515:39.

85. There is a difference of opinion regarding whether one would have to wait *kedei sheyaaseh* in this case. Based on note 74, the enactment would seem to apply here according to Rashi but not according to Tosafos, since there is no danger of one Jew asking another to do work for him on Yom Tov.

86. HaGaon Rav Shlomo Zalman Auerbach explains that although the second day of Yom Tov is a rabbinic enactment, it is treated like the first day. In his responsa at the end of *Shemiras Shabbos KeHilchasah*, HaGaon Rav Auerbach writes that even according to those who rule that the prohibition against *melachah* on Chol HaMoed is rabbinic, one may not derive benefit on Chol HaMoed from *melachah* performed on Chol HaMoed.

CHAPTER 2
Specific Festival Observances

Pesach

1. The *maariv* service for Yom Tov is recited on the second night of Pesach. In communities where *Hallel* is recited with its blessings on the first night of Pesach, it is also recited on the second night.[1] One who mistakenly recited the weekday *Shemoneh Esrei* has not fulfilled his obligation until he recites the *Shemoneh Esrei* of Yom Tov.[2]

2. After *maariv*, before reciting *Aleinu*, one begins to count the Omer.[3]

---

1. *Shulchan Aruch* 487:4; *Mishnah Berurah* 473:1; *Shaar HaTziyun* 473:3. Also see chapter 1, paragraph 2.

2. *Magen Avraham* 268:2; *Mishnah Berurah* 268:10.

3. *Shulchan Aruch* 489:1; *Mishnah Berurah* 489:2.
   The counting of the Omer coincides with the offering of the Omer in the Beis HaMikdash on the second day of Pesach, the first day of Chol HaMoed in Eretz Yisrael. Although in Chutz LaAretz the second day of Pesach is still Yom Tov, the blessing over counting the Omer is recited, despite the apparent contradiction. In contrast, the Gemara concludes that since Shemini Atzeres may be the seventh day of Sukkos, one should sit in the sukkah but refrain from reciting the blessing. It follows, therefore, that the blessing over counting the Omer should also be omitted. Moreover, every time one counts the Omer, it would seem that two days should be counted because of the doubt as to on which day the count should have begun.

3. The second Seder should be conducted exactly like the first.[4] *Yaaleh VeYavo* is inserted in *birkas hamazon*, just as it is for the remainder of the holiday.[5]

4. Wheat, barley, oats, rye, or spelt planted after Pesach may not be eaten until the eighteenth of the following Nisan (which begins at night following the second day of Yom Tov). In Eretz Yisrael, the "new" grain may be eaten on the seventeenth of Nisan (the night following the first day).[6] Many authorities rule that this prohibition applies even when the Beis HaMikdash is not standing and even

---

The Baal HaMaor, at the end of *Pesachim*, offers the following solution: "In the case of Shemini Atzeres the blessing, which should be said because of the rabbinic enactment of Yom Tov Sheini, cannot uproot Shemini Atzeres, which is not considered Sukkos according to Torah law. In the case of counting the Omer on the second night of Pesach, however, the blessing—which emanates from the first day of Yom Tov, a Torah Law, cannot be uprooted by the rabbinic enactment of Yom Tov Sheini." See *Devar Avraham*, vol. 1, no. 34:3; *Minchas Elazar*, vol. 1, no. 65; *Doveiv Meisharim*, vol. 1, no. 15; *Shaar HaTziyun* 489:51.

4. Rema, *Orach Chaim* 481:2. Also see *Teshuvos Chasam Sofer, Orach Chaim*, no. 15.

5. *Birkas hamazon* must be repeated if one omits *Yaaleh VeYavo* on Yom Tov (see *Halichos Bas Yisrael*, English edition, p. 117, note 39, concerning a woman who omits *Yaaleh VeYavo* on Yom Tov), but not if one omits it on Chol HaMoed.

Hissorerus Teshuvah (vol. 1, no. 61) concludes that in this matter Yom Tov Sheini has the same status as the first day of Yom Tov.

6. This prohibition, known in Hebrew as *chadash*, is based on Vayikra 23:14, "And bread and toasted grains you shall not eat until this very day, until you offer the sacrifice of HaShem [the Omer]; this shall be an everlasting statute throughout your generations in all your dwelling places." Any grain planted before Pesach became permitted with the offering each Pesach.

Since the second day of Yom Tov may actually be the first day, we are stringent with regard to *chadash* on that day as well. See *Shulchan Aruch, Yoreh Deah* 293; and *Mishnah Berurah* 489:44.

outside of Eretz Yisrael.[7] Others are lenient,[8] which is the prevalent custom in the Diaspora.

5. On the last two nights of Pesach, Kiddush is recited without the *shehecheyanu* blessing.[9] In communities where Kiddush is recited in the synagogue, the Omer is counted afterward.[10]

6. It is forbidden to eat *chametz* on the eighth day of Pesach. Among those who are accustomed not to eat matzah soaked in water (*gebrochts*) during Pesach, some act leniently on the eighth day,[11] while others act stringently on this day as well.[12]

---

7. *Shulchan Aruch, Orach Chaim* 489:10 and *Yoreh Deah* 293:1-2. This ruling is based on the concluding words of the verse cited in note 6—"an everlasting statute throughout your generations in all your dwelling places." The Bach, in his glosses on *Yoreh Deah*, defends the many people who are lenient regarding this law, but the Vilna Gaon and the Shaagas Aryeh (in *Kuntres Dinei Chadash*) both conclude that all the later authorities have shown his arguments to be baseless. The Mishnah Berurah (489:45) states that although one should not criticize those who are lenient, every God-fearing person should act stringently whenever possible. Also see the Bei'ur Halachah, who proves that according to most Rishonim *chadash* today is forbidden by Torah law while according to others it is at least a rabbinic prohibition.

In recent years, many American *b'nei Torah* have begun to act stringently in this matter. Today it is possible to ascertain which products contain *chadash* and at which times of the year they are marketed. In most Jewish communities, it is also possible to purchase non-*chadash* baked goods.

8. Those who are lenient rely on the Bach, who maintains that *chadash* applies only in Eretz Yisrael.

9. *Shulchan Aruch* 490:7; *Mishnah Berurah* ad loc.

10. *Mishnah Berurah* 490:43, in the name of the Pri Megadim and the Chayei Adam, who reject the view of the Taz that the counting of the Omer should precede Kiddush.

11. The Rema (*Orach Chaim* 467:8) notes that although certain communities do not eat dried, sugared fruits during Pesach lest they contain *chametz*, they may be lenient on the eighth day since—according to the Mishnah Berurah—it is highly unlikely that these fruits do contain *chametz*. *Chok Yaacov* (491) adds that we are lenient on the eighth day with respect to many stringencies.

In *Birkas Pesach* 16, HaGaon Rav Pinchas HaLevi Horovitz cites the words of *Derech Pikudecha*: "Any practice observed on Pesach over and above the strict dictates of the law should not be observed on the eighth day. Otherwise, one implies that he considers [the stringency] required by law." *Hagahos Pischa Zuta* notes that

7. A person who finds *chametz* in his home on the first day of Pesach may not destroy it on Yom Tov. The *chametz* is *muktzeh*; it may not even be removed from the house. The *chametz* should be covered with a utensil until after Yom Tov Sheini, at which time it should be burned.[13]

8. Food in which a tiny of amount of *chametz* was mixed on the eighth day of Pesach may be kept in the house and eaten after Yom Tov.[14]

Shavuos

9. The regular Yom Tov prayers are recited on the second day of Shavuos.[15]

---

the author of *Toras Chaim* observed stringencies on the eighth day of Pesach until Kabbalists arrived from Eretz Yisrael and exclaimed, "Over there [in Eretz Yisrael] they are eating *chametz* and you are still observing *chumros*?!" Also see *Sdeh Chemed, Maareches Chametz U'Matzah* 6:7; *Minchas Elazar*, vol. 3, no. 43.

12. *Birkas Pesach* (16) notes that the Pri Chadash and the Chida both treated the eighth day like the rest of the holiday. *Hanhagos Chofetz Chaim*, printed in vol. 3 of *Kisvei Chofetz Chaim*, states, "My father did not eat kneidelach or soaked matzah on Pesach. My mother's uncle, an elderly, distinguished gentleman, once visited our home on the last day of Pesach, and she made kneidelach in his honor. My father also tasted the dish, out of respect for his guest."

The Magen Avraham (446:2) rules that if one finds a product containing *chametz* on the eighth day of Pesach, he may keep it, even though it would have to be destroyed if found during the rest of the holiday. Also see *Bei'ur Halachah* 448, s.v. "*Afilu*," in the name of the Pri Chadash.

13. *Shulchan Aruch* 446.

14. *Shulchan Aruch* 467:10; *Mishnah Berurah* 467:44. Normally, when treife food becomes mixed with kosher food and the kosher food is sixty times' the volume of the treife food, the mixture is deemed kosher. During Pesach, the rabbis suspended this principle of *bitul beshishim* and even the tiniest amount of *chametz* makes the mixture forbidden. On the last day of Pesach, however, *bitul beshishim* applies. If more than one-sixtieth of a mixture is *chametz*, however, the mixture is forbidden.

15. See paragraph 1.

Shavuos is unique among the holidays in that the Torah does not specify its date, only that it is celebrated fifty days after the beginning of the counting of the Omer. Since by the end of these fifty days, the Jews in the Diaspora certainly knew which day Pesach actually began, there was no doubt about which day was Shavuos. Why, then, is it necessary to observe a second day of Shavuos in the Diaspora?

10. Certain Sephardic communities are accustomed to stay awake on both nights of Shavuos. Although Ashkenazim are not so accustomed, they should still study Torah on the second night.[16]

Rosh HaShanah

11. Two days of Rosh HaShanah are observed both in Eretz Yisrael and in Chutz LaAretz.[17]

Rambam (*Hilchos Kiddush HaChodesh* 3:12) explains that Chazal did not wish to differentiate between the holidays; they therefore enacted a second day of Shavuos despite the absence of any doubt. *Teshuvos Chasam Sofer* (*Orach Chaim*, no. 145) concludes from this statement that the observance of the second day of Shavuos is actually stricter than Yom Tov Sheini on other holidays since it is based not on doubt but on a definite rabbinic enactment. See *Teshuvos Chasam Sofer, Yoreh Deah*, no. 252; *Machazeh Avraham*, no. 121; *Meshech Chochmah, Bemidbar* 29:12; and *Chiddushei Maran HaRiz HaLevi, parashas Emor*.

16. The Kaf HaChaim (*Orach Chaim* 494:10) states: "On the second night of Shavuos, one should also set aside time for Torah study. What happened to the Beis Yosef on the second night of Shavuos is well known [the Shelah, p. 180, reports that the *Shechinah* spoke to the Beis Yosef and Rav Shlomo Alkabitz on the second night of Shavuos]....Happy is he who stays awake and studies Torah on the second night of Shavuos as well." See *Yesod VeShoresh HaAvodah, Shaar Teshi'i*, chap. 10.

17. *Shulchan Aruch* 601:2. Since Rosh HaShanah occurs on the first day of the month of Tishrei, Jews in Eretz Yisrael were also in doubt as to which day the Sanhedrin had declared Rosh Chodesh. Furthermore, even in Yerushalayim there were years when two days were observed:

Rabban Yochanan ben Zakai decreed that witnesses should not be accepted in the afternoon. When they did not arrive in the morning on the thirtieth day of Elul, it was clear that Rosh HaShanah was the next day, but an additional decree required people to observe both days as Yom Tov—the first, since it had begun to be observed in case the witnesses came; and the second, as the actual day of Rosh HaShanah (*Beitzah* 5a).

The above situation clarifies the concept of *kedushah achas*, according to which the two days of Rosh HaShanah are halachically considered one long day. Whereas other Yamim Tovim are observed for two days because of the doubt as to which day is actually Yom Tov, Rosh HaShanah was sometimes observed for two days even though there was no such doubt. The ramifications of *kedushah achas* are referred to throughout chapter 1. For further details, see *Mishnah Berurah* 601:3; *Sho'eil U'Meishiv, Mahadurah Tlisai*, vol. 2, no. 85; and *Chazon Ish, Orach Chaim*, no. 131.

Yom Kippur

12. One day of Yom Kippur is observed even in Chutz LaAretz.[18]

Sukkos

13. The order of prayers and Kiddush is identical on the first two nights of Sukkos,[19] except that on the second night *shehecheyanu* is recited before the blessing of *leisheiv basukkah*.[20]

14. One is obligated to recite Kiddush and eat at least a *kezayis* of bread in the sukkah on the second night of Sukkos.[21] If it is raining, he should wait for the rain to stop and then eat in the sukkah. If

---

18. Rema, *Orach Chaim* 624; *Mishnah Berurah* 624:7. Certain outstanding individuals in previous generations observed two days of Yom Kippur. The Mishnah Berurah outlines the halachic details pertaining to this practice.

19. This is also the case on the first and second nights of Shavuos (paragraph 9). See paragraph 17 as to why *shehecheyanu* is not recited when taking the *lulav* on the second day of Yom Tov.

    Mishnah Berurah (660:5), citing the Magen Avraham, reports that some people are mistakenly accustomed to eat a new fruit on the second night of Yom Tov and bear the fruit in mind when they say *shehecheyanu*. See, however, *Eliyah Rabbah* 645:1 and *Bikurei Yaacov* 641:4, which justify this practice.

20. *Shulchan Aruch* 661:1. On the first night of Sukkos, *shehecheyanu* is said for both the holiday and the sukkah. It is therefore recited after the blessing over the sukkah. On the second night, however, *shehecheyanu* is only recited for the holiday, in case the first day was not actually Yom Tov. Consequently, there should be no interruption between Kiddush and *shehecheyanu*. (Even if the first day is not actually Yom Tov, the *shehecheyanu* recited that night is valid for the sukkah; in fact, even if one recited the blessing when he finished building his sukkah, he fulfilled his obligation.)

    The Mishnah Berurah (641:2) notes that one may adopt the opposing view of the Radvaz and the Maharshal, who concur with *Avi Ezri* that *shehecheyanu* is recited after the blessing over the sukkah on the second night as well. But if many people are eating together, they should all follow the same opinion. See *Maasei Rav*, under the laws of Sukkos; and *Amudei Ohr*, no. 36.

21. The obligation to eat a *kezayis* of bread only applies on the first two nights of Sukkos in the Diaspora. During the rest of the holiday, if one eats bread he must eat it in the sukkah, but there is no obligation to eat bread.

one cannot wait,[22] he may recite Kiddush in his home, but later he should eat a *kezayis* of bread in the sukkah, omitting *leisheiv basukkah* and *shehecheyanu* if it's still raining.[23]

15.   One who forgot to recite *shehecheyanu* on the second night of Sukkos may do so the next day whenever he remembers, even before Kiddush.[24]

16.   During *mussaf* on the second day, the sacrifice brought on the

---

22. The Mishnah Berurah (639:2) cites authorities who rule that one should wait until midnight for the rain to stop. But he concludes that if waiting so long will interfere with the joy of the holiday [i.e., his wife and children do not wish to stay up so late], it is sufficient to wait an hour or two.

23. The Rema (*Orach Chaim* 639:5) cites authorities who rule that although one is exempt from sitting in the sukkah in inclement weather, this exemption does not apply to the special mitzvah of eating a *kezayis* of bread in the sukkah on the first night. The Mishnah Berurah notes that others apply the exemption to this mitzvah as well. He concludes that if it rains on the first night, one should recite Kiddush and eat a *kezayis* of bread in the sukkah, in accordance with the Rema. However, since there is a dispute over whether the mitzvah applies, the blessing of *leisheiv basukkah* should be omitted.

   With respect to the second night of Yom Tov, the Magen Avraham (639:5) infers from the words of the Rema that one need not eat in the sukkah if it is raining. The text therefore states that on the second night one may act leniently and recite Kiddush in the house. Nevertheless, the Taz (639:10) cites other authorities who obligate a person to eat a *kezayis* of bread in the sukkah on the second night as well.

24. Although *shehecheyanu* is recited as part of Kiddush, it refers to the entire holiday. Thus, if a person omitted the blessing during Kiddush on the first night, it may be said anytime the next day. Once the second day of Yom Tov begins, however, it should not be said until Kiddush. If it was omitted on the second night as well, it may be said anytime during the holiday, even on the last day.

   The Mishnah Berurah (473:1) applies this ruling to one who recited *shehecheyanu* on the first night but omitted it on the second night; he, too, should recite the blessing whenever he remembers, even during Chol HaMoed or the concluding days of the holiday. In *Shaar HaTziyun*, however, an opposing view is cited in the name of *Mor U'Ketziah* and *Nehar Shalom*: since *shehecheyanu* on the second night was enacted only so that people should not treat the second day lightly because of its rabbinic nature, if it was not said on the second day of Yom Tov, it is not to be recited during Chol HaMoed. *Shaar HaTziyun* fails to reach a definitive conclusion in this matter. Also see *Bei'ur Halachah* 529, s.v. "*BeErev Yom Tov*," and 543, s.v. "*VeAchar Kach*;" and *Bikurei Yaacov* 662:2.

first day is mentioned. If the sacrifice of the second day was mentioned, *mussaf* must be repeated.[25]

The Four Species

17. Every day of Sukkos, the blessing of *al netilas lulav* is recited upon taking the four species.[26] *Shehecheyanu*, however, is only recited on the first day of Yom Tov,[27] unless it is Shabbos, in which case the mitzvah is fulfilled for the first time—and *shehecheyanu* is said—on the second day of Yom Tov.[28]

18. If a set of four species is kosher but does not meet the requirements of the first day of Sukkos—e.g., it doesn't belong to the person fulfilling the mitzvah[29]—it may be used on the second day, but the blessing of *al netilas lulav* should be omitted.[30]

---

25. *BeTzeil HaChochmah*, vol. 2, no. 68:6. If a person only said, "as it states in Your Torah," without describing the offering of either day, he has fulfilled his obligation.

26. *Shulchan Aruch* 662:1. According to Torah law, the *lulav* is taken in the Beis HaMikdash each day of Sukkos and outside the Beis HaMikdash only on the first day. As a remembrance of the way the mitzvah was fulfilled in the Beis HaMikdash, the rabbis decreed that today the four species should be taken every day of Sukkos, with a blessing. See *Mishnah Berurah* 662:1.

27. *Shulchan Aruch* 662:2. The Mishnah Berurah (662:2) cites the ruling that one who recites *shehecheyanu* when binding the four species together before Yom Tov does not repeat it the first time he fulfills the mitzvah during Sukkos. Likewise, when one recites *shehecheyanu* on the first day he does not repeat it on the second day, even if the first day was not actually Yom Tov. In contrast, because the *shehecheyanu* recited during Kiddush refers to the sanctity of the day, each day of Yom Tov requires a separate *shehecheyanu*.

28. A person recites *shehecheyanu* the first time he takes the four species during Sukkos, even if he does not fulfill the mitzvah until the last day of the festival. See *Mishnah Berurah* 662:3.

29. The different requirements when taking the four species on the first day, when it is a Torah law, and the rest of the festival, when it is a rabbinic enactment, are detailed in *Shulchan Aruch* 649.

30. *Shulchan Aruch* 649:5. The Mishnah Berurah (649:50) bases this ruling on the dispute over whether the defects that invalidate the four species on the first day of Sukkos apply on the second day as well.

However, this ruling only applies if a set suitable for the first day is not readily obtainable.[31]

One who has a proper set may give it to someone else as a gift on condition that it be returned. The recipient may then recite the blessing over that set[32] but use his own during *Hallel*.[33]

19. After taking the four species on the first day of Yom Tov, one should not give them to a child for him to fulfill the mitzvah.[34] If one did, he may not recite the blessing over them on the second day.[35] It is best to purchase a separate set of four species for one's child.[36]

However, the Bei'ur Halachah (s.v. "*Pesulei*") cites the Bikurei Yaacov in the name of the Eliyah Rabbah, the Pri Megadim, and others, who insist that one may not recite a blessing over a borrowed set of four species on the second day of Yom Tov, since one cannot fulfill the mitzvah with such a set on the first day.

31. *Mishnah Berurah* 649:50. This leniency even applies on the first day of Sukkos, but only if a suitable set is completely unavailable.

32. *Mishnah Berurah* 649:51. A *matanah al menas lehachzir*, a gift given on condition that it be returned, is a legal mode of transfer. As long as the recipient fulfills the condition and returns the object, it legally belonged to him while it was in his possession, provided that he made a formal *kinyan*, such as lifting it.

33. Ibid.

34. Although minors can acquire objects, they are halachically incapable of transferring possession to others. Therefore, if a man gives his *lulav* to a minor before performing the mitzvah, he will be unable to reacquire it in order to fulfill his obligation (*Shulchan Aruch* 658:6). The Mishnah Berurah (558:23) applies this rule to one who observes two days of Yom Tov as well; he should not give his *lulav* to a minor on the first day of Sukkos, even after he has fulfilled the mitzvah, since he must reacquire it for the second day.

35. *Mishnah Berurah* 558:23. Authorities dispute whether a child above the age of six or seven can transfer possession to another party. *Bei'ur Halachah* (s.v. "*Lo Yitnenu*") recommends that one not transfer title of his *lulav* to a child of any age, even conditionally.

36. The Magen Avraham (658:5) cites the Rosh, who maintains that a parent does not fulfill his obligation to teach his child about taking the four species unless the child owns a set. The Pri Megadim concludes that, according to this view, once a child is old enough to fulfill the mitzvah, his parent must purchase a kosher set for him.

Nevertheless, many people rely on the view[37] that a child may borrow his father's set.

Shemini Atzeres

20. On the eighth day of Sukkos, one recites the *Shemoneh Esrei* and Kiddush for Shemini Atzeres, not Sukkos.[38]

Birkei Yosef (657:2) rules that since the second day of Yom Tov is rabbinic, a parent can fulfill the mitzvah of *chinuch* on that day by lending his child a set. The Netziv (*Meishiv Davar*, vol. 3, no. 41) explains that the Birkei Yosef would permit the child to recite the blessing over a borrowed set on the second day of Yom Tov, but the Netziv himself disagrees.

HaGaon Rav Moshe Feinstein (*Iggeros Moshe, Orach Chaim*, vol. 3, no. 95) sides with the Magen Avraham. He notes that in Europe it was customary to be lenient because of the prevalent poverty and scarcity. Today, however, when God has blessed us with His bounty and a kosher set of four species is relatively inexpensive, a parent should purchase one for each of his children, thereby fulfilling the mitzvah of *chinuch* in the best way possible.

37. *Mishnah Berurah* 658:28, citing the Mordechai in the name of the Raavan.

In his glosses on the *Shulchan Aruch*, HaGaon Rav Shlomo Kluger cites the Chacham Tzvi (no. 9), who notes that the mitzvah of taking the four species is twofold: the Torah obligation applies only on the first day and requires that the four species be owned by the person fulfilling the mitzvah; the rabbinic obligation applies all seven days and is fulfilled even if the person does not own the four species. The Chacham Tzvi explains that if one takes four species that do not belong to him on the first day, although he does not fulfill the Torah obligation, he does fulfill the rabbinic one. Although this view may not be used to justify the recitation of a blessing over a borrowed *lulav* on the first day, many people rely on it regarding the mitzvah of *chinuch*. HaGaon Rav Shlomo Zalman Auerbach has explained that although it is preferable to do as stated in note 36, one should not object to those who rely on the Chacham Tzvi.

38. The rabbinic enactment that Shemini Atzeres be treated as the seventh day of Sukkos based on doubt does not supersede its Torah-mandated sanctity. If one mentioned Sukkos in his *Shemoneh Esrei* but did not yet recite the blessing of "*Mekadesh Yisrael vehazemanim*," he should return to the words "*VaTitein lanu*" and continue from there. The Mishnah Berurah (668:2) cites differing opinions as to whether a person must repeat the *Shemoneh Esrei* if he realized his error after concluding it.

21. One should not begin the evening meal of Shemini Atzeres until nightfall.[39] If a person accidentally washed his hands for the meal before nightfall, he should not recite the blessing of *leisheiv basukkah.*[40]

22. The Shemini Atzeres meals should be eaten in the sukkah, but without reciting the blessing of *leisheiv basukkah.*[41] Some authorities rule that one should sleep in the sukkah on Shemini Atzeres,[42] but others state that one should not.[43] The lenient view is accepted in practice.[44]

Foods that need not be eaten in the sukkah during Sukkos, such as fruit and water,[45] may be eaten either in or out of the

---

39. *Mishnah Berurah* 668:7. It is halachically unclear whether twilight is part of the incoming day (Shemini Atzeres, on which the blessing of *leisheiv basukkah* is not recited) or the outgoing day (the seventh day of Sukkos, on which the blessing is recited). By waiting until nightfall, one avoids this dilemma.

Shaar HaTziyun (668:11) adds that even if a person recited the *maariv* of Shemini Atzeres before sunset, it is forbidden to eat the Yom Tov meal until nightfall.

40. *Mishnah Berurah* 668:7.

41. *Sukkah* 47b. The Rif and Rosh explain that reciting the blessing would contradict the mention of Shemini Atzeres in one's prayers. Tosafos, the Ran, and the Tur add that it would constitute a degradation of the holiday.

42. *Mishnah Berurah* 668:6 and *Shaar HaTziyun* 668:4, in the name of the Beis Yosef and the Vilna Gaon; and *Bikurei Yaacov*, in the name of the Rashba, *Rosh HaShanah* 16a. One is not guilty of adding onto the Torah (*bal tosif*) by sleeping in the sukkah on Shemini Atzeres since he does not intend to add to the time prescribed by the Torah. In fact, *Chayei Adam* (153:5) reports that the Vilna Gaon was extremely particular to sleep in the sukkah on Shemini Atzeres, even if it was very cold outside.

43. The Mordechai, citing the Raviyah, maintains that although one who sleeps in the sukkah does not technically transgress *bal tosif*, he may appear to be doing so. Eating in the sukkah bears no such semblance of *bal tosif* since no blessing is recited beforehand, unlike the rest of the week. Since no blessing is ever recited over sleeping in the sukkah, however, there is nothing to distinguish sleeping there on Shemini Atzeres from doing so throughout the week; it therefore seems as though one is adding to the mitzvah.

44. *Mishnah Berurah* 668:6.

45. See the *Shulchan Aruch* 639:2 and *Mishnah Berurah* ad loc. for a full discussion of which foods may be eaten outside the sukkah during Sukkos.

sukkah, even by those who insist on eating them in the sukkah during Sukkos.[46]

23. After the afternoon meal, it is customary to leave the sukkah for the rest of the day. But if one wishes to eat another meal later, it must be eaten in the sukkah.[47]

24. The four species are not taken on Shemini Atzeres.[48] Nevertheless, the *esrog* may not be eaten until Simchas Torah.[49] Although some authorities forbid eating the *esrog* on Simchas Torah when it occurs on Sunday,[50] most do not.[51]

---

46. The Mishnah Berurah (668:6) explains that, according to the Raviyah cited in note 43, foods over which the blessing of *leisheiv basukkah* is not recited should not be eaten in the sukkah on Shemini Atzeres, lest one create the impression of *bal tosif*. But *Shaar HaTziyun* (668:9), citing *Bikurei Yaacov*, maintains that since one is not obligated to eat these foods in the sukkah, the Raviyah would concede that doing so on Shemini Atzeres does not seem as though one is adding to the mitzvah.

47. *Mishnah Berurah* 668:5.

48. See Tosafos, *Sukkah* 47a, s.v. "*Meisav.*"

49. *Shulchan Aruch* 665:1. Since the *esrog* was designated for the fulfillment of a mitzvah, it is *muktzeh machmas mitzvah*, i.e., it may not be used for another purpose until this mitzvah is no longer in effect. This does not occur until Simchas Torah, for Shemini Atzeres may or may not be the seventh day of Sukkos.

50. Ibid.; *Mishnah Berurah* 665:6. Since it was forbidden to use the *esrog* on Shabbos, the *esrog* was considered "unprepared" before Shabbos for use on Shabbos. If it would be used the next day, it would appear to have been "prepared" on Shabbos for Yom Tov.

51. *Shulchan Aruch* 665:1; *Mishnah Berurah* 665:5. These authorities maintain that the prohibition of preparing on Shabbos for Yom Tov only applies when something comes into existence on Shabbos (such as an egg laid on Shabbos) or when a person prepares physically.

CHAPTER 3
Visiting Eretz Yisrael on Yom Tov Sheini

Introduction

1. According to most authorities, a ben Chutz LaAretz (a resident of Chutz LaAretz)[1] who is visiting Eretz Yisrael observes all the laws of Yom Tov Sheini.[2] Some rule that such a visitor follows the custom of Eretz Yisrael and observes one day of Yom Tov.[3] A third opinion requires the visitor to adopt the stringencies of both

---

1. A detailed halachic definition of permanent residence is given later in this book.

2. This is the view of the Beis Yosef (*Avekas Rocheil*, no. 26), which is accepted by *Shaarei Teshuvah* (496), *Birkei Yosef* (496), *She'eilas Yaavetz* (vol. 2, no. 168), *Pe'as HaShulchan* (*Hilchos Eretz Yisrael* 2:15), and *Mishnah Berurah* (496:13). Also see *Teshuvos Chasam Sofer, Yoreh Deah*, no. 252, regarding Rashi, *Pesachim* 47a.

3. *Chacham Tzvi* (no. 167) argues that the obligation to observe Yom Tov Sheini depends on where a person is spending Yom Tov, not where he permanently resides. Not only is a Jew who visits Eretz Yisrael exempt from Yom Tov Sheini, but, in his view, he is forbidden to observe it. This opinion is cited in *Shulchan Aruch HaRav* (*Orach Chaim* 496).

Yom Tov and weekday.⁴ The consensus among contemporary authorities follows the first opinion.⁵

---

4. *Ir HaKodesh VeHaMikdash* (vol. 3, 19:11) reports that HaGaon Rav Shmuel Salant was wont to rule in accordance with the Chacham Tzvi, as cited in note 3. HaGaon Rav Salant found support for this view in the reason we observe Yom Tov Sheini today, after the establishment of the calendar: "Preserve the traditions of your forefathers" (*Beitzah* 4a). Therefore, today we should act exactly as our forefathers acted before the establishment of the calendar. In those days, a visitor to Eretz Yisrael certainly was not obligated to observe Yom Tov Sheini, so he should be exempt nowadays as well. (HaGaon Rav Moshe Feinstein, in *Iggeros Moshe, Orach Chaim*, vol. 3, no. 73, counters that the observance of Yom Tov Sheini is more stringent today than it was in ancient times since it is observed even though we are no longer in doubt as to which day is Yom Tov.)

Nevertheless, HaGaon Rav Salant did not rule conclusively in favor of the Chacham Tzvi because of the opposing view of his teacher, the Pe'as HaShulchan, cited in note 2. Instead, he maintained that a visitor should observe the stringencies of both views:

a. Following the first day of Yom Tov, he should recite the weekday *Shemoneh Esrei*, including the Havdalah prayer, "*Atah Chonantanu.*" He should listen to a ben Eretz Yisrael recite Havdalah and he should not recite Kiddush.

b. On the first day of Chol HaMoed Sukkos (Yom Tov Sheini in Chutz LaAretz), he should recite the weekday *Shemoneh Esrei*, adding *Yaaleh VeYavo*. During *mussaf* he should recite the verses describing the sacrifice brought on the second day of the festival, not the first, as is customary in Chutz LaAretz. He may be called to the Torah but should refrain from all *melachah* forbidden on Yom Tov.

c. On Shemini Atzeres he should not sit in the sukkah and he may be called to the Torah. Following Shemini Atzeres, he should recite the weekday *maariv*, omitting *Yaaleh VeYavo*. He should listen to Havdalah recited by a ben Eretz Yisrael and he should not recite Kiddush.

d. The next day (Simchas Torah in Chutz LaAretz), he should lay tefillin and recite the weekday *Shemoneh Esrei* but refrain from *melachah*.

e. Following the first day of Pesach, he should listen to Havdalah recited by a resident of Eretz Yisrael and he should not recite Kiddush. Although HaGaon Rav Salant was not in favor of the visitor making a second Seder, one who wishes to do so should eat a *kezayis* of matzah and *marror* without reciting the appropriate blessings over these mitzvos. He may drink the four cups of wine, but the blessing should only be recited over the first and third cups. The Haggadah may be recited, but the blessing at the end of the *Maggid* section should be omitted.

f. Following the seventh day of Pesach, he should not eat *chametz* or do any *melachah*, but he should lay tefillin and recite the weekday prayers.

g. When Yom Tov occurs on Thursday (and Yom Tov Sheini is on Friday) and he is cooking his own food, he should set aside an *eiruv tavshilin* without reciting the blessing.

Davening with the Congregation

2. It is customary for visitors to Eretz Yisrael to form their own minyan on Yom Tov Sheini.[6]

---

5. HaGaon Rav Moshe Feinstein, *Iggeros Moshe, Orach Chaim,* vol. 4, no. 101; *Minchas Yitzchak,* vol. 4, nos. 1-4, and vol. 9, no. 54; and *Shaarei Yitzchak,* introduction, citing the Chazon Ish and the Gaon of Tchebin. This is also the conclusion of HaGaon Rav Shlomo Zalman Auerbach, HaGaon Rav Yosef Shalom Eliashiv, HaGaon Rav Shmuel HaLevi Wosner, and HaGaon Rav Chaim Pinchus Scheinberg. I have heard from HaGaon Rav Ben Tziyon Abba Shaul that this is the Sephardic custom as well. (See chapter 8 concerning one who is single.)

HaGaon Rav Eliashiv has explained to me that since the Chacham Tzvi's son, HaGaon Rav Yaacov Emden, rejects his father's view in *She'eilas Yaavetz* (vol. 2, no. 168), it may no longer be relied on, even when other factors indicate that a person is exempt from observing Yom Tov Sheini. This is also implicit in the works of HaGaon Rav Feinstein. However, HaGaon Rav Auerbach and many other contemporary authorities maintain that although we do not follow the Chacham Tzvi, his view may be used as a deciding factor when there are differences of opinion or other reasons to be lenient. See *Moadim U'Zemanim,* vol. 7, no. 120, in the notes citing HaGaon Rav Reuven Bengis. This is also the approach taken by HaGaon Rav Ben Tziyon Abba Shaul in determining the halachah for the Sephardic community.

6. *Kaf HaChaim* (*Orach Chaim* 496:38), citing Rav Yosef Karo (*Avekas Rocheil,* no. 26), reports that this was the practice in early times and no authorities ever objected. Also see *Pe'as HaShulchan, Hilchos Eretz Yisrael* 2:15. Although the Mishnah Berurah (496:130) states that one should pray in private, he refers to an individual visiting Eretz Yisrael, for if he would recite the Yom Tov prayers in public it would cause dissension. The Mishnah Berurah presumably would not have the same objection to a group of Chutz LaAretz residents forming their own minyan. Although some authorities in previous generations opposed this practice, HaGaon Rav Yosef Shalom Eliashiv concludes that we may rely on Avekas Rocheil since this has been the custom for so many years. HaGaon Rav Shlomo Zalman Auerbach adds that since this practice has become so widespread, people who observe one day of Yom Tov understand the reason for the separate minyan; consequently, no dissension results. Although *Teshuvos HaRadvaz* (vol. 4, no. 73) requires a ben Eretz Yisrael visiting Chutz LaAretz to recite the weekday *Shemoneh Esrei* silently, this ruling only applies in Chutz LaAretz, where it is not customary for residents of Eretz Yisrael to form a separate minyan and it may lead to dissension. This is also the conclusion of HaGaon Rav Ben Tziyon Abba Shaul, who notes that in Rav Yosef Karo's day, many people came to Eretz Yisrael for Yom Tov and everyone knew that they observed two days. Nevertheless, HaGaon Rav David Feinstein has told me that although his father, HaGaon Rav Moshe Feinstein, did not forbid this practice since it has become established, he did not advocate it.

3. A ben Chutz LaAretz who mistakenly recited the weekday *Shemoneh Esrei* on Yom Tov Sheini must go back and recite the Yom Tov one instead.[7]

Eiruv Tavshilin

4. If Yom Tov Sheini occurs on Friday, a ben Chutz LaAretz who plans on cooking for Shabbos on Friday must set aside an *eiruv tavshilin* before Yom Tov.[8] If he does not plan on cooking—for example, if he is a guest—he should set aside the *eiruv* without reciting the blessing, in order to be permitted to light Shabbos candles.[9]

5. If his host is to be his agent in setting aside the *eiruv*, a ben Chutz LaAretz may give him either some of his own bread and a cooked dish, or food given to him by his host.[10] But the host may not use his own food to set aside an *eiruv* on behalf of his guest.[11]

6. If a ben Chutz LaAretz forgot to set aside an *eiruv tavshilin*

---

7. This is based on a ruling by HaGaon Rav Shlomo Zalman Auerbach. As stated in note 5, the Chacham Tzvi's view may be used as an additional factor only when the halachah is in doubt, whereas in this case a ben Chutz LaAretz is *undoubtedly* obligated to recite the Yom Tov *Shemoneh Esrei* on the second day, so there is no room to be lenient.

8. A ben Chutz LaAretz is obligated to observe all the laws of Yom Tov as practiced in Chutz LaAretz, including *eiruv tavshilin*. See chapter 1, paragraph 8, for details.

9. The *Shulchan Aruch* (527:19) cites a dispute over whether an *eiruv tavshilin* is needed to light Shabbos candles. The Mishnah Berurah (527:55) concludes that an *eiruv* is required. But *Kaf HaChaim* (*Orach Chaim* 496:113), *Minchas Yitzchak* (vol. 7, no. 36), and *Shemiras Shabbos KeHilchasah* (31:83), in the name of HaGaon Rav Shlomo Zalman Auerbach, all rule that if an *eiruv* is set aside only to permit candlelighting, no blessing should be recited.

10. *Chaim She'al*, vol. 1, no. 74; *Shaarei Yitzchak* 14:8, citing *Artzos HaChaim*. Also see *Be'er Moshe*, pp. 200-201. *Chaim She'al* questions, however, whether a ben Eretz Yisrael may recite the blessing on behalf of a visitor, since he is not obligated in the mitzvah.

11. *Chaim She'al*, vol. 1, no. 74.

until Yom Tov Sheini,[12] he is forbidden to cook or perform any preparations for Shabbos.[13] It is also forbidden for a ben Eretz Yisrael to cook a ben Chutz LaAretz's food for him, even if he cooks it in his own home.[14] But the guest may ask his host to cook for him if the food belongs to the host.[15] Alternatively, the guest may give his food to his host and ask him to cook it for him.[16]

With regard to candlelighting, the ben Chutz LaAretz should give his candles to a ben Eretz Yisrael to light on his behalf. If this is impossible, he may light one candle for Shabbos and recite the blessing.[17]

If another ben Chutz LaAretz has set aside an *eiruv tavshilin* on behalf of all the visitors in the city, he may rely on that *eiruv* for both cooking and candlelighting.[18]

---

12. If he remembered on the first day of Yom Tov, he may set aside an *eiruv* on that day and recite the following: "If today is actually Yom Tov, no *eiruv* is necessary. If tomorrow is Yom Tov, through this *eiruv* may it be permitted for us to bake, cook...." See *Shulchan Aruch* 527:22 and chapter 1, note 32. This conditional declaration may not be used on the first day of Rosh HaShanah.

13. A person who did not set aside an *eiruv* is only permitted to bake one loaf of bread and cook one food item. See *Shulchan Aruch* 527:20.

Normally one who forgets to set aside an *eiruv* may rely on the one prepared by the rabbi of the city for all the local residents. In this case, however, the Jews of the city only observe one day of Yom Tov, so no *eiruv* was set aside for them.

14. *Shulchan Aruch* 527:20 and *Mishnah Berurah* ad loc.

15. The host may only add the guest's food to a dish he is cooking for himself; he may not cook him a special dish unless the host also intends to partake of it. See *Shulchan Aruch* 527:21 and *Shemiras Shabbos KeHilchasah* 31:84.

16. *Shulchan Aruch* 527:20 and *Mishnah Berurah* ad loc. Whenever the guest must "give" his food to his host, a formal method of acquisition must be used—the host must lift up the food, etc., with intent to acquire it. See *Shaarei Yitzchak* 4:3, 14:4.

17. See note 9. The Kaf HaChaim (*Orach Chaim* 527:112) maintains that if lighting only one candle will diminish one's enjoyment of Shabbos, he may rely on the opinion that no *eiruv* is required for lighting Shabbos candles and he may light his usual number of candles.

18. *Shulchan Aruch* 527:7 and the second paragraph of note 13. This applies only if the one who set aside the *eiruv* first "gave" it to all these visitors through a formal mode of acquisition, as explained in the *Shulchan Aruch*.

Sukkos

7. A ben Chutz LaAretz may use an *aravah*[19] (willow branch) that was uprooted by a ben Eretz Yisrael on Yom Tov Sheini,[20] even if he has another *aravah* but prefers a freshly picked one;[21] the other species may not be used if they were picked on Yom Tov Sheini.[22]

8. Most authorities require a ben Chutz LaAretz to sit in the sukkah on Shemini Atzeres without reciting the blessing, just as he would in Chutz LaAretz.[23] This is the accepted custom. Other authorities exempt him from this obligation.[24]

---

19. See *Mishnah Berurah* 655:3. In Chutz LaAretz, an *aravah* is *muktzeh* if picked on Yom Tov Sheini, even by a non-Jew.

20. HaGaon Rav Shlomo Zalman Auerbach explains that such an *aravah* is *muktzeh* only in Chutz LaAretz, where Yom Tov is observed by everyone. But in Eretz Yisrael, where most Jews are allowed to pick an *aravah* on Yom Tov Sheini, it is not *muktzeh* for visitors from Chutz LaAretz either. See the responsa of HaGaon Rav Auerbach in the appendix of the Hebrew edition of *Yom Tov Sheini KeHilchaso*. HaGaon Rav Yosef Shalom Eliashiv agrees with this ruling, but *Minchas Yitzchak* (vol. 8, no. 59) concurs only where no other *aravah* is available.

A ben Chutz LaAretz may not pick out or buy the *aravah* himself, however. He must either receive it as a gift from a ben Eretz Yisrael or pay for it in advance. Alternatively, he may hint to a ben Eretz Yisrael (in a permissible manner—see chapter 14, note 3) that he should purchase the *aravah* for him, and then receive it from him as a gift.

21. This is based on the ruling of HaGaon Rav Shlomo Zalman Auerbach.

22. *Aravos* are commonly picked during Chol HaMoed but the other species are not; hence, if picked on Yom Tov Sheini, they are *muktzeh* for residents of Chutz LaAretz.

23. *Be'er Moshe*, p. 217. This is also the view of HaGaon Rav Yosef Shalom Eliashiv, HaGaon Rav Shmuel HaLevi Wosner, and HaGaon Rav Chaim Pinchus Scheinberg. HaGaon Rav Ben Tziyon Abba Shaul relates that this is the Sephardic custom as well.

24. HaGaon Rav Y. M. Tokichinsky, *Luach Eretz Yisrael*; HaGaon Rav Shlomo Zalman Auerbach as quoted in *Shemiras Shabbos KeHilchasah* 31, note 92; *Minchas Shlomo*, no. 19. *Minchas Yitzchak* (vol. 9, no. 54) adds that sitting in the sukkah on Shemini Atzeres may constitute a public deviation from the local custom. In contrast, residents of Chutz LaAretz are permitted to form their own minyan on Yom Tov Sheini because this practice has been done for generations and will not lead to dissent (see *Avekas Rocheil*, no. 26). Also see the view of the Chacham Tzvi, cited in note 3.

9. A ben Chutz LaAretz may participate in the *hakafos* of Sim-chas Torah, even though for him it is Shemini Atzeres.[25]

Giving Gifts

10. A ben Chutz LaAretz may present a gift to a ben Eretz Yisrael[26] as long as he does not participate in the formal act of acquisition.[27] But he should not accept a gift from a ben Eretz Yisrael unless it is to be used for a mitzvah, such as for the Shabbos meals.[28] In special cases a halachic authority should be consulted.[29]

HaGaon Rav Yosef Shalom Eliashiv rules that if a pot or some other inappro-priate utensil is placed in the sukkah, even a ben Eretz Yisrael could eat there (see *Shulchan Aruch* 666:1). Thus, there is really no issue of defying local custom when a ben Chutz LaAretz does so.

25. This is the widespread practice in Eretz Yisrael today. Rav Ephraim Greenblat has written me that this is how HaGaon Rav Moshe Feinstein instructed him to act when he visited Eretz Yisrael in 5711.

HaGaon Rav Shlomo Zalman Auerbach rules that a ben Chutz LaAretz may participate in a *simchas beis hashoeivah* on Yom Tov Sheini, even if there is live music.

26. *BeTzeil HaChochmah* (vol. 3, no. 123) cites *Sefer HaMakneh*, which states that a person may give a gift on Shabbos and Yom Tov but it is rabbinically forbidden to receive one. This is also the view of *Chochmas Shlomo* (655), *Mahari Assad*, (*Orach Chaim*, no. 83), *Kesav Sofer* (*Orach Chaim*, no. 59), and others. Since, in this case, the second day is not Yom Tov for the recipient, there is no prohibition against giving the gift.

27. *BeTzeil HaChochmah*, vol. 3, no. 123. An object is acquired either by the recipient drawing it to him (*meshichah*) or by the giver giving a handkerchief to the recipient, which is then returned to him (*kinyan sudar*). *BeTzeil HaChochmah* infers from Rambam that the prohibition does not apply to the giver (see note 26) because he performs no action. If he would participate in the transfer, such as in the case of *kinyan sudar*, the prohibition would apply to him as well.

28. *Magen Avraham* 306:15.

29. *BeTzeil HaChochmah* (vol. 3, no. 123) notes that: *Beis Meir* (*Even HaEzer*, no. 45) limits the prohibition against giving gifts on Yom Tov to immovable objects; *Binyan Shlomo* (*Orach Chaim*, no. 17) permits one to receive a gift if he does not intend to formally acquire it; and *Maharshag* (vol. 2, no. 103) forbids only gifts that cannot be used without further preparation. A rav should be consulted as to when these minority views may be relied upon.

Litigation

11. A ben Chutz LaAretz may appear in rabbinical court on Yom Tov Sheini if he cannot reschedule the trial before he departs from Eretz Yisrael.[30] This applies even if both litigants live in Chutz LaAretz but the case is heard by a court in Eretz Yisrael.[31]

Hosting Non-Observant Jews on Yom Tov Sheini

12. A ben Eretz Yisrael who is hosting non-observant guests from abroad need not stop them from performing *melachah* on Yom Tov Sheini, unless they are acting on his behalf.[32]

---

30. *BeTzeil HaChochmah*, vol. 1, no. 65. The rabbis decreed that a *din Torah* should not be conducted on Shabbos and Yom Tov lest the judges write down their verdict. Thus, if it is not Yom Tov for the judges, the case may be heard on Yom Tov Sheini. This is the also the conclusion of *Be'er Moshe* (pp. 259-260). *Chelkas Yaacov* (vol. 3, no. 135), however, concludes that litigating on Yom Tov diminishes the sanctity of the day, especially nowadays, when people tend to treat Yom Tov Sheini lightly. *BeTzeil HaChochmah* responds to these arguments in vol. 2, no. 79, but concludes that the reader may choose which opinion to rely upon. HaGaon Rav Shlomo Zalman Auerbach agrees with *BeTzeil HaChochmah* that, since the litigant observes all the other laws of Yom Tov Sheini, appearing in court does not degrade the sanctity of the day.

31. *BeTzeil HaChochmah*, vol. 1, no. 65. This is also the ruling of HaGaon Rav Shlomo Zalman Auerbach.

32. HaGaon Rav Shlomo Zalman Auerbach emphasizes that the host must ascertain that his guest observed the first day of Yom Tov only out of respect for him. Therefore, if he sees his host performing *melachah* on the second day, it is unlikely that he himself will agree not to. Concerning a rabbinic prohibition such as this, "better one should transgress unintentionally than intentionally." But if the guest observes Yom Tov and will listen when he is told to observe Yom Tov Sheini, the host is obligated to inform him.

CHAPTER 4
Visiting
Chutz LaAretz on
Yom Tov Sheini

Melachah

1. Wherever Jews reside in Chutz LaAretz,[1] a ben Eretz Yisrael may
not perform *melachah* on Yom Tov Sheini[2]—even if he intends to

---

1. *Mishnah Berurah* 496:2, based on *Chullin* 110a. Once a person comes within the
techum Shabbos (2,000 cubits) of a Jewish settlement, he must adopt its stringencies.
See *Be'er Moshe*, p. 148; and *Minchas Yitzchak*, vol. 4, no. 2:21-22.

HaGaon Rav Shlomo Zalman Auerbach and HaGaon Rav Yosef Shalom Eliashiv rule that a ben Eretz Yisrael may not perform *melachah* on Yom Tov Sheini
even if the Jews in the city are not observant.

2. *Pesachim* 50a cautions against following one's own lenient custom when visiting
a place that has adopted more stringent practices, lest he cause dissent. Nevertheless, HaGaon Rav Shlomo Zalman Auerbach distinguishes between the observance
of Yom Tov Sheini and other customs. With respect to other customs, one is only
required to observe the practice of an established Jewish community. Yom Tov
Sheini, however, which has been accepted all over the Diaspora, must be observed
wherever Jews live, even where there is no organized community.

64

return to Eretz Yisrael immediately after Yom Tov.[3] This prohibition applies to actions forbidden by either Torah law or rabbinic injunction.[4] The consensus of contemporary authorities is to forbid *melachah* even in private.[5]

If the visitor spends Yom Tov Sheini in a place where there are no Jews,[6] he may perform *melachah*.[7]

In *Iggeros Moshe* (*Orach Chaim*, vol. 4, no. 104), HaGaon Rav Moshe Feinstein remains undecided about whether a visitor from Eretz Yisrael may turn on a light on Yom Tov Sheini. HaGaon Rav Auerbach, however, forbids a ben Eretz Yisrael to perform such an act, which (according to many authorities) is based on the rabbinic prohibition of bringing something into being. Furthermore, according to the Taz (*Orach Chaim* 402:1), this prohibition is in fact a Torah law. This also appears to be Ramban's view (*Milchamos HaShem, Beitzah* 24b). Moreover, the Chazon Ish (*Orach Chaim* 50:9) rules that by completing an electric circuit, one transgresses the Torah prohibition of *boneh* (building).

3. *Shulchan Aruch* 496:3. See chapters 5-8 for a discussion of how one determines his status with regard to Yom Tov Sheini.

4. See note 1 in the name of HaGaon Rav Shlomo Zalman Auerbach and HaGaon Rav Yosef Shalom Eliashiv. HaGaon Rav Eliashiv adds that a ben Eretz Yisrael may not handle *muktzeh*, even in private, nor may he ask a non-Jew to perform *melachah* for him.

5. *Magen Avraham* 496:4; *Chayei Adam* 103:4. Although with respect to other customs, a visitor may act leniently in private, Yom Tov Sheini is treated with more stringency due to its universal nature.

It should be noted that the Taz (*Orach Chaim* 496:2) cites the Maharshal, who permits a ben Eretz Yisrael to perform *melachah* privately on Yom Tov Sheini. This is also the view of *Mahari Tatz* (no. 139), *Avekas Rocheil* (no. 26), as explained in *Yechaveh Daas* (vol. 3, no. 35), and the Mabit (vol. 3, no. 149). But *Mishnah Berurah, Shulchan Aruch HaRav,* and *Aruch HaShulchan* follow the majority, as do *Iggeros Moshe* (vol. 3, no. 72), HaGaon Rav Shlomo Zalman Auerbach, HaGaon Rav Yosef Shalom Eliashiv, and HaGaon Rav Shmuel HaLevi Wosner. HaGaon Rav Ben Tziyon Abba Shaul reports that the Sephardim are stringent as well.

HaGaon Rav Auerbach denounces those who are lenient in this matter. He further writes, "There has been an increase in the number of people who take Yom Tov Sheini lightly. If a ben Eretz Yisrael performs *melachah* on Yom Tov Sheini [even in private], there is a danger that it will strengthen those who degrade the sanctity of the day."

6. *Shulchan Aruch* 496:3. A ben Eretz Yisrael must refrain from *melachah* on Yom Tov Sheini to avoid dissent; this reason does not apply if there are no Jews where he is spending Yom Tov. See *Mishnah Berurah* 496:10.

7. See *Shulchan Aruch* 468:4 and *Magen Avraham* ad loc. concerning other customs.

2. A ben Eretz Yisrael who moves to Chutz LaAretz[8] is considered a ben Chutz LaAretz as soon as he reaches any settlement outside Eretz Yisrael, even if no Jews live there.[9] Even if he subsequently finds himself in an uninhabited area,[10] he must observe Yom Tov Sheini.[11]

3. Some authorities permit a ben Eretz Yisrael to fly to Chutz LaAretz on Yom Tov Sheini, even if he will arrive at an airport within the boundaries of a city in which Jews reside.[12] Others insist that the airport be outside the city's *techum Shabbos* (2,000 cubits).[13] All authorities forbid him to enter the city itself until after Yom Tov Sheini.[14]

4. Some authorities permit hotel guests from Eretz Yisrael to perform *melachah* on Yom Tov Sheini in the presence of other Jews if:

---

8. See chapters 5-8.

9. *Mishnah Berurah* 496:2, which also cites *Bigdei Yesha*'s view that a person remains a ben Eretz Yisrael until he arrives at a place where other Jews live.

10. *Shulchan Aruch* 496:3; *Mishnah Berurah* 496:12.

11. *Shulchan Aruch* 496:3, in accordance with the Baal HaMaor. Raavad maintains that once a person leaves Eretz Yisrael with intent to move to Chutz LaAretz, he immediately becomes a ben Chutz LaAretz, even before arriving anywhere.

12. HaGaon Rav Shlomo Zalman Auerbach explains that although there are probably many non-observant Jews in the airport at any given time, an airport has a different status than a city where Jews reside. Since people arrive there from all over the world, including Eretz Yisrael, if one Jew sees another arrive on Yom Tov Sheini, he will assume he came from Eretz Yisrael and it will not lead to dissent.

13. *BeTzeil HaChochmah*, vol. 3, no. 35; and *Be'er Moshe*, p. 149. This is also the ruling of HaGaon Rav Yosef Shalom Eliashiv and HaGaon Rav Ben Tziyon Abba Shaul. HaGaon Rav Eliashiv, however, stipulates that if Jews—even non-observant ones—work in the airport at all times, a Jew may not fly in on Yom Tov Sheini. He concludes that one must investigate this matter thoroughly before setting out on his journey.

Be'er Moshe further notes that if a person is well-known and news of his arrival on Yom Tov Sheini will spread to the city, he may not arrive on that day.

14. *BeTzeil HaChochmah*, vol. 1, no. 66. Although once one enters the city after Yom Tov Sheini everyone will realize that he arrived on Yom Tov, the Sages were only concerned about dissent on Yom Tov itself, not afterward.

a) the hotel is located outside a city where Jews live;

b) the owner of the hotel is not Jewish; and

c) the hotel is only kosher on Yom Tov[15] and Jews do not stay there the rest of the year.[16]

Prayer

5. A ben Eretz Yisrael visiting Chutz LaAretz should recite "*Atah Chonantanu*" (the Havdalah prayer) during *maariv* on the night of Yom Tov Sheini.[17] It is proper to attend synagogue services that evening and the following afternoon,[18] but people should not realize that he is reciting the weekday *Shemoneh Esrei*.[19]

6. On the concluding day of the festival[20] a ben Eretz Yisrael

---

15. Both HaGaon Rav Shlomo Zalman Auerbach and HaGaon Rav Yosef Shalom Eliashiv rule that if the hotel is kosher the entire year, it is considered a Jewish settlement. The fact that different groups of people stay there the rest of the year is irrelevant.

16. According to HaGaon Rav Shlomo Zalman Auerbach, since Jews do not stay at the hotel the rest of the year, it is not considered a place where Jews reside. Moreover, because the guests are aware that these people live in Eretz Yisrael, their conduct will not lead to dissent. And since the hotel is not kosher, we discount the possibility that Jews may visit during the rest of the year. HaGaon Rav Yosef Shalom Eliashiv, however, rules that *melachah* is only permitted if no Jews, even non-observant ones, stay there the rest of the year.

17. *Mishnah Berurah* 496:13. HaGaon Rav Moshe Feinstein rules (in *Iggeros Moshe*, *Orach Chaim*, vol. 3, no. 72) that he should recite Havdalah only in *Shemoneh Esrei*, not over a cup of wine. Although normally one may not eat before reciting Havdalah over wine, in this situation, one may. Most authorities require that Havdalah be recited in private, however, and according to them one may not eat beforehand.

18. This is the view of HaGaon Rav Shlomo Zalman Auerbach. According to HaGaon Rav Yosef Shalom Eliashiv, however, he is *required* to attend synagogue services. See note 24 for a full discussion.

19. See the view of the Pri Chadash cited in note 23.

    Melamed Lehoil (*Orach Chaim*, no. 110) states that if he wishes, he may conclude the blessing before *Shemoneh Esrei* with the words "*u'feros aleinu*" (as is normally said on Yom Tov) instead of the weekday conclusion of the blessing, "*Shomeir amo Yisrael la'ad*."

20. This rule also applies on the second day of Pesach and Sukkos for those who are accustomed to wear tefillin on Chol HaMoed.

should put on tefillin privately[21] and recite *kerias Shema* while wearing them.[22] Some authorities rule he should then remove his tefillin and go to shul to recite the *Shemoneh Esrei* with the congregation.[23] Others maintain that he should recite the *Shemoneh Esrei* privately, while still wearing tefillin.[24] Afterward, he may go to shul to hear *Kaddish, Kedushah,* and *Barechu.*[25]

---

21. *Mishnah Berurah,* 496:13.

22. The Gemara (*Berachos* 14b) states that a person who recites *kerias Shema* without tefillin bears false witness about himself, since the mitzvah of tefillin is mentioned in the Shema.

23. The Pri Chadash (496:25, cited in *Chayei Adam* 101:64 and *Kaf HaChaim, Orach Chaim* 669:35) reports that when he visited Egypt, he put on tefillin privately, recited *kerias Shema,* and then removed them and went to shul to recite the *Shemoneh Esrei* with the congregation, without making it apparent that he was reciting the longer, weekday version. HaGaon Rav Yosef Shalom Eliashiv also rules that it is only essential to wear tefillin for *kerias Shema;* reciting *Shemoneh Esrei* with the congregation takes precedence over saying the prayer while wearing tefillin. As indicated in the words of the Pri Chadash, one fulfills the mitzvah of communal prayer even if he recites a different *Shemoneh Esrei.*

24. *Shemiras Shabbos KeHilchasah* 31, note 89, in the name of HaGaon Rav Shlomo Zalman Auerbach. Citing the *Shulchan Aruch* 66 and *Mishnah Berurah* 66:40, HaGaon Rav Auerbach considers it more important to recite the *Shemoneh Esrei* while wearing tefillin than to pray with the congregation, especially when it recites a Yom Tov *Shemoneh Esrei* and the ben Eretz Yisrael recites a weekday one, in which case he may not even fulfill the mitzvah of *tefillah betzibbur.* And no proof can be brought from the case of the Pri Chadash since he was well-known and would have been missed had he not attended services. See *Shaarei Yitzchak* 10:3, and *Melamed Lehoil, Orach Chaim,* no. 110.

HaGaon Rav Auerbach's argument for reciting *Shemoneh Esrei* at home only applies to *shacharis,* when tefillin are worn. Even on the second day of Pesach and Sukkos, when many people do not wear tefillin, HaGaon Rav Auerbach does not require a ben Eretz Yisrael to go to shul. He does, however, suggest attending *minchah* and *maariv* to hear *Kaddish* and *Kedushah,* provided that no one realizes he is reciting a different *Shemoneh Esrei.* HaGaon Rav Moshe Feinstein (in *Iggeros Moshe, Orach Chaim,* vol. 3, no. 92) also writes that a ben Eretz Yisrael is only required to attend services if he will be missed. This implies that he does not have to fulfill the mitzvah of *tefillah betzibbur*—in accordance with the view of HaGaon Rav Auerbach.

25. HaGaon Rav Ben Tziyon Abba Shaul advises one to attend services in order to hear *Kaddish, Kedushah,* and *kerias HaTorah,* especially on Simchas Torah, when *VeZos HaBerachah* is read. Otherwise, he will miss that *parashah* completely.

If the person will be missed by the congregants, he is *required* to go to shul and appear to participate.[26]

7.   Visitors from Eretz Yisrael may not form a separate minyan on Yom Tov Sheini.[27]

Dress

8.   A ben Eretz Yisrael visiting Chutz LaAretz must dress formally on Yom Tov Sheini.[28]

Eiruv Tavshilin

9.   If Yom Tov Sheini occurs on Friday, a ben Eretz Yisrael may cook for Shabbos without setting aside an *eiruv tavshilin*.[29] But he may not bathe or cut his nails in honor of Shabbos.[30] He should light candles on

---

26. *Iggeros Moshe, Orach Chaim*, vol. 3, no. 92. Also see note 24 in the name of HaGaon Rav Shlomo Zalman Auerbach.

27. *Avekas Rocheil*, no. 26. This ruling is also indicated in *Teshuvos HaRadvaz* (vol. 4, no. 73) and *Pri Chadash* (496). *Har Tzvi* (vol. 2, no. 78) questions whether they may make a minyan for *maariv* when Yom Tov Sheini falls on Shabbos. Although the only difference in the prayer service is *Shemoneh Esrei*, which is recited silently, this, too, may constitute a degradation of Yom Tov. HaGaon Rav Shlomo Zalman Auerbach and HaGaon Rav Yosef Shalom Eliashiv prohibit such a minyan even if no local residents will discover it. Forming a separate minyan in Eretz Yisrael is only permitted because this practice has been established over centuries (see chapter 3, note 6). No such tradition exists in Chutz LaAretz. This is also the ruling of HaGaon Rav Ben Tziyon Abba Shaul for Sephardic visitors to Chutz LaAretz.

   Kaf HaChaim (*Orach Chaim* 669:33) notes that the Chida forbade a group of Jews from Eretz Yisrael to celebrate *hakafos* on Shemini Atzeres. HaGaon Rav Auerbach and HaGaon Rav Eliashiv concur with this view. Also see *BeTzeil HaChochmah*, vol. 1, no. 66.

28. *Teshuvos HaRadvaz*, vol. 27, no. 73; *Mishnah Berurah* 496:13.

29. Radvaz, cited by the Magen Avraham (496:7), Mishnah Berurah, and other authorities. Since no one knows that he did not set aside an *eiruv tavshilin*, this does not constitute a degradation of Yom Tov.

30. This is the ruling of HaGaon Rav Shlomo Zalman Auerbach. Since these preparations involve *melachah*, they are forbidden even privately.

the night of Yom Tov Sheini, omitting the blessing.[31]

Pesach

10. A ben Eretz Yisrael need not conduct a second Seder.[32] If he is staying with residents of Chutz LaAretz, he should either attend their Seder and recite the Haggadah with them[33] or, preferably, tell them he's attending a Seder elsewhere.[34]

11. A ben Eretz Yisrael who participates in a second Seder should ask a ben Chutz LaAretz to recite Kiddush for him.[35] He may recite the blessing of *Borei pri hagafen* over the first and third cups of wine but should ask a ben Chutz LaAretz to recite the blessings over the second and fourth cups for him,[36] as well as the blessing *asher*

---

31. *Iggeros Moshe, Orach Chaim,* vol. 3, no. 72. HaGaon Rav Shlomo Zalman Auerbach rules that he should light candles even if no residents of Chutz LaAretz are staying with him, for if someone comes to visit and sees no Yom Tov candles burning, this may result in a degradation of Yom Tov.

32. *Chayei Adam* 103:4.

33. Ibid.

34. This is HaGaon Rav Shlomo Zalman Auerbach and HaGaon Rav Yosef Shalom Eliashiv's interpretation of the Chayei Adam.

If he is visiting his immediate family and no other guests or relatives are expected to arrive, he may sit with them without participating in the Seder. But if other guests are expected, he may not excuse himself.

Nevertheless, HaGaon Rav Ben Tziyon Abba Shaul notes that among Sephardim, a ben Eretz Yisrael does not participate in the second Seder and this is not considered a degradation of Yom Tov.

35. *Iggeros Moshe, Orach Chaim,* vol. 3, no. 72. Listening to another person's blessings as opposed to reciting them oneself does not constitute a degradation of Yom Tov, provided that one express his desire to fulfill his "obligation."

36. *Chayei Adam,* 103:4. A separate blessing is recited over the second and fourth cups of wine because the recitation of *Maggid* and *Hallel* are interruptions between the first and second cups and between the third and fourth cups, respectively. Since the guest is not obligated to recite these passages, they are not interruptions for him. (See *Shaarei Yitzchak* 10:3.) *Iggeros Moshe (Orach Chaim,* vol. 3, no. 72), however, cites the Vilna Gaon, who bases these blessings on the prohibition against drinking

ge'alanu at the end of *Maggid.*[37] He should eat the matzah and *marror*, omitting the blessings of *al achilas matzah* and *al achilas marror*. He need not eat a *kezayis* of *marror.*[38]

12. A ben Eretz Yisrael who spends Pesach in Chutz LaAretz is forbidden to eat *chametz* on the eighth day of Pesach, even privately.[39]

Shemini Atzeres

13. A ben Eretz Yisrael visiting Chutz LaAretz should sit in the sukkah with his hosts on Shemini Atzeres but without intending to fulfill the mitzvah. Furthermore, he should take some food normally eaten in the sukkah and eat it outside the sukkah when no one is looking. If his host sleeps in the sukkah, he should find some excuse to sleep in the house.[40]

14. If some of the city's observant Jews eat in their homes on Shemini Atzeres, some authorities rule that the guest may eat in the house as well.[41]

---

during *Maggid* and *Hallel*. Accordingly, since a ben Eretz Yisrael may also not drink at these times, he is also required to recite the blessings over the second and fourth cups. In view of this controversy, it is best for a ben Eretz Yisrael to listen to someone else recite them.

37. See note 35.

38. *Iggeros Moshe, Orach Chaim*, vol. 3, no. 72. Because people will not realize he is eating less than the required amount, it will not lead to a degradation of Yom Tov.

39. *Aruch HaShulchan* 496:5.

40. *Shaarei Teshuvah* 668:3, citing *Birkei Yosef.*

41. There are different customs concerning sitting in the sukkah on Shemini Atzeres. Some eat all their meals there, others only recite Kiddush there, others eat only the evening meal there and still others eat there only in the morning. HaGaon Rav Shlomo Zalman Auerbach limits the ruling of the Birkei Yosef, cited in note 40, to a city that has one fixed practice. If the visitor eats in the house in a place where there are different customs, no degradation of Yom Tov will result, for people will assume that this is his custom.

Immersion in a *Mikvah*

15. A woman from Eretz Yisrael who must immerse in the *mikvah* on the second night of Yom Tov should cut her fingernails and perform all other preparations before Yom Tov, even if this means preparing on Chol HaMoed.[42] Preferably, however, a non-Jewish woman should cut her fingernails on the night of her immersion.[43]

---

42. HaGaon Rav Shlomo Zalman Auerbach explains that although she is cutting her fingernails on Chol HaMoed in preparation for immersing after Yom Tov, this is not the kind of preparation forbidden on Chol HaMoed. Since we follow the Magen Avraham, who forbids a guest from Eretz Yisrael to perform *melachah* on Yom Tov Sheini (even privately), cutting her fingernails on Chol HaMoed avoids a potential degradation of Yom Tov and is therefore necessary for the holiday. In addition, some authorities permit the cutting of fingernails on Chol HaMoed in any case, while others permit it if the fingernails were cut before Yom Tov. See the *Shulchan Aruch* 632:1.

43. This is based on a ruling by HaGaon Rav Shlomo Zalman Auerbach. If she forgot to cut her fingernails before Yom Tov and no non-Jew is available to cut them for her on the night of Yom Tov Sheini, HaGaon Rav Auerbach has written me that "perhaps she should postpone her immersion, although [in this situation] she may be permitted to cut her fingernails in absolute privacy."

CHAPTER 5
A Permanent Change of Residence

(This chapter has been written for a ben Chutz LaAretz who moves to Eretz Yisrael, but the same laws apply to a ben Eretz Yisrael who moves to Chutz LaAretz, unless otherwise indicated.)

1. A ben Chutz LaAretz who moves to Eretz Yisrael becomes a ben Eretz Yisrael as soon as he arrives,[1] even if he will return to Chutz LaAretz before Yom Tov to collect his family.[2]

2. A ben Chutz LaAretz who decides to remain in Eretz Yisrael during a visit there becomes a ben Eretz Yisrael as soon as his decision is final.[3]

---

1. *Shulchan Aruch* 496:3. *Avnei Neizer* (*Orach Chaim*, no. 424:34) questions whether he becomes a ben Eretz Yisrael immediately or only after living in Eretz Yisrael for a year. The above halachah follows the view of *Minchas Yitzchak* (vol. 4, no. 4) and *BeTzeil HaChochmah* (vol. 1, no. 6), which corresponds to the plain meaning of the *Shulchan Aruch*. This is also the conclusion of HaGaon Rav Shlomo Zalman Auerbach.

2. *Minchas Yitzchak*, vol. 4, no. 4:56; *BeTzeil HaChochmah*, vol. 1, no. 6, in the name of *Shaarei Teshuvah* 496:5 and *Chochmas Adam* 52; *Kaf HaChaim*, *Orach Chaim* 143.

3. *Minchas Yitzchak*, vol. 4, no. 4:56.

3. If a ben Chutz LaAretz moves to Eretz Yisrael, finds a home and employment, and then decides to move back to Chutz LaAretz, he remains a ben Eretz Yisrael until he actually returns.[4]

4. A ben Chutz LaAretz who is in the process of moving to a particular city in Eretz Yisrael is considered a ben Eretz Yisrael upon arrival in the country, even before he reaches his final destination.[5]

5. If a ben Chutz LaAretz spends Yom Tov in Eretz Yisrael and decides to settle there during Yom Tov Sheini, some authorities rule that he immediately becomes a ben Eretz Yisrael and does not continue observing Yom Tov.[6] According to this view, he should say Havdalah, put on tefillin, and recite the weekday *Shemoneh Esrei*.[7] Other authorities require him to observe the remainder of Yom Tov Sheini.[8]

6. If a ben Eretz Yisrael spends Yom Tov in Chutz LaAretz and

---

4. This is based on a ruling by HaGaon Rav Shlomo Zalman Auerbach. If he decides to move back before finding a home and employment, he should consult a halachic authority.

5. This is based on a ruling by HaGaon Rav Shlomo Zalman Auerbach and HaGaon Rav Yosef Shalom Eliashiv. Since all of Eretz Yisrael has the same status, he becomes a ben Eretz Yisrael as soon as he reaches a populated area.

6. This is the view of HaGaon Rav Shlomo Zalman Auerbach and *Minchas Yitzchak* (vol. 7, no. 34).

7. This refers to the last day of Yom Tov, and to the second day for those who lay tefillin during Chol HaMoed.

8. *Minchas Elazar*, vol. 3, no. 59; *BeTzeil HaChochmah*, vol. 1, no. 53.

HaGaon Rav Yosef Shalom Eliashiv rules that if he decides to remain in Eretz Yisrael in the evening or morning, he need not observe the rest of Yom Tov. But if he makes his decision after most of Yom Tov Sheini is over, he must observe Yom Tov for the rest of the day. See *Kovetz Shiurim, Beitzah*, no. 16.

Be'er Moshe (p. 175) stipulates that if his decision was based on factors that existed before Yom Tov began, it becomes clear retroactively that he never meant to accept Yom Tov Sheini; consequently he is not required to observe it. If his decision was based on new factors, however, his acceptance of Yom Tov Sheini remains binding.

decides to settle there during Yom Tov Sheini, he immediately becomes a ben Chutz LaAretz.[9]

7. A ben Chutz LaAretz who decides to move to Eretz Yisrael remains a ben Chutz LaAretz until he arrives in the country.[10]

---

9. *Minchas Yitzchak*, vol. 4, no. 5, citing *Shevus Yaacov*, vol. 1, no. 40, and *Imrei Binah, Hilchos Shabbos*, no. 11. This is also the ruling of HaGaon Rav Yosef Shalom Eliashiv and HaGaon Rav Shmuel HaLevi Wosner, but HaGaon Rav Shlomo Zalman Auerbach is doubtful. Although the Rosh (*Moed Katan* 3:96) rules that a child who becomes bar mitzvah in the middle of Shabbos is immediately obligated to observe the day, this may only apply to Shabbos, a Torah law. But the rabbinic enactment of Yom Tov Sheini may only apply to those who were obligated at the onset of the day.

10. *Iggeros Moshe, Orach Chaim*, vol. 4, no. 108. Every Jew anxiously awaits the coming of Mashiach and the opportunity to move to Eretz Yisrael, yet he must still observe Yom Tov Sheini. HaGaon Rav Elazar Menachem Shach (*Iggeros U'Kesavim*, vol. 3) concurs. HaGaon Rav Shlomo Zalman Auerbach rules further that even if a person took an oath to move to Eretz Yisrael, his status does not change until he actually moves.

CHAPTER 6
Temporary
Resettlement

Introduction

As stated, a visitor remains a resident of his place of origin with respect to Yom Tov Sheini. But contemporary authorities differ about a person who resettles temporarily. The following laws are extremely complex and most situations are not identical to those described below. In most cases, a halachic authority must be consulted.

In this chapter we deal with one who resettles with his family. The status of a single person will be discussed in chapter 8.

Like chapter 5, this chapter has been written for a ben Chutz LaAretz who travels to Eretz Yisrael. Unless otherwise indicated, the same laws apply to a ben Eretz Yisrael who travels to Chutz LaAretz.

Changing Residence

1. A ben Chutz LaAretz who travels to Eretz Yisrael and plans to

return to a new home in a different city in Chutz LaAretz is still considered a ben Chutz LaAretz.[1]

A Visitor Who is Forced to Remain

2. A ben Eretz Yisrael who is forced to extend his stay in Chutz LaAretz indefinitely[2] is considered a ben Chutz LaAretz, even if he intends to return to Eretz Yisrael as soon as possible.[3]

If circumstances change and he is able to return to Eretz Yisrael but not before Yom Tov, some authorities rule that he regains his original status.[4] But if he had despaired of ever returning to Eretz Yisrael, he remains a ben Chutz LaAretz until he actually returns.[5]

---

1. This is the view of HaGaon Rav Shlomo Zalman Auerbach (*Minchas Shlomo*, no. 19) and HaGaon Rav Yosef Shalom Eliashiv. All of Chutz LaAretz is viewed as one place. But see *Mikraei Kodesh*, Pesach 58:2.

2. For example, if he became involved in legal proceedings barring his return to Eretz Yisrael. See *Minchas Yitzchak*, vol. 5, no. 43, concerning a ben Eretz Yisrael who cannot return home because of his wife's objections.

HaGaon Rav Isser Zalman Meltzer, cited in *Shaarei Tziyon*, discusses the case of a ben Chutz LaAretz who was trapped in Eretz Yisrael during World War II: "It is difficult to determine if he is still a ben Chutz LaAretz. Nevertheless, he should certainly refrain from *melachah* and not eat *chametz* on the eighth day of Pesach." I have heard from HaGaon Rav Shlomo Zalman Auerbach, however, that such a person is certainly considered a ben Chutz LaAretz.

3. HaGaon Rav Shlomo Zalman Auerbach explains that since he may be forced to stay in Chutz LaAretz for years, he follows the local custom. *Minchas Yitzchak* (vol. 5, no. 43), however, advises such a person to recite the weekday *Shemoneh Esrei* and put on tefillin without reciting the blessing, but to refrain from *melachah* on Yom Tov Sheini and make an *eiruv tavshilin*.

HaGaon Rav Yosef Shalom Eliashiv notes that this rule only applies if he has no means of returning to Eretz Yisrael. But if he has, and has no intention of staying in Chutz LaAretz, he remains a ben Eretz Yisrael.

4. This is the view of HaGaon Rav Shlomo Zalman Auerbach and HaGaon Rav Yosef Shalom Eliashiv. According to HaGaon Rav Nissim Karelitz, however, he remains a ben Chutz LaAretz until he actually returns.

5. This is even according to HaGaon Rav Shlomo Zalman Auerbach in note 4.

Extended Stays

Introduction

According to the Aruch HaShulchan, a ben Chutz LaAretz who comes to Eretz Yisrael for a year or more and intends to return to Chutz LaAretz afterward is nonetheless considered a ben Eretz Yisrael the moment he arrives in the country.[6] Most authorities rule that he remains a ben Chutz LaAretz.[7] The laws described below follow the latter opinion. According to the Aruch HaShulchan, in all these situations, one follows the local custom.

Relocating with One's Family

3. Early authorities ruled that a ben Chutz LaAretz who comes to Eretz Yisrael with his family, even for a short period, is considered a ben Eretz Yisrael throughout his stay.[8] Contemporary authorities attribute this ruling to the great difficulties once involved in travel, in which case one who journeyed to Eretz Yisrael with his family presumably intended to remain there. Today, however, when travel is much easier, there is no such presumption and one remains a ben Chutz LaAretz until he decides to settle in Eretz Yisrael.[9]

---

6. *Shulchan Aruch* 496:5; *Avnei Neizer, Orach Chaim*, no. 424:34. This ruling is based on *Bava Basra* 7b: "How long must one reside in a city to be considered a resident? Twelve months." Also see *She'eilas Yaavetz*, no. 168; *Seridei Eish*, vol. 2, no. 161; *Tzitz Eliezer*, vol. 9, no. 30:3; *Yechaveh Daas*, vol. 3, no. 35; and HaGaon Rav Shmuel HaLevi Wosner, *Shevet HaLevi, Yoreh Deah*, no. 65.

7. This ruling can be inferred from *Magen Avraham* (468:12) and *Mishnah Berurah* (496:13). This is also the position of HaGaon Rav Moshe Feinstein (*Iggeros Moshe, Orach Chaim*, vol. 3, no. 75), HaGaon Rav Shlomo Zalman Auerbach, HaGaon Rav Chaim Pinchus Scheinberg, and most contemporary authorities, as cited below.

8. *Teshuvos HaRadvaz* (no. 1073) writes that one who travels from Eretz Yisrael to Chutz LaAretz with his wife, even for a short stay, has uprooted his home and is considered as if he does not intend to return. This ruling is cited in *Magen Avraham* (496:7) and *Mishnah Berurah* (496:13).

Relocating for the Purpose of Torah Study

4. Some authorities rule that if a ben Chutz LaAretz comes to Eretz Yisrael with his family to study Torah for a few years and is prepared to remain there if he can earn a livelihood, he is immediately considered a ben Eretz Yisrael.[10] Others maintain that he remains a ben Chutz LaAretz until he definitely decides to settle in Eretz Yisrael.[11] A third opinion considers him a ben Eretz Yisrael but recommends that he not perform *melachah* on Yom Tov Sheini or eat *chametz* on the eighth day of Pesach.[12] Once he decides to settle in Eretz Yisrael, all agree that he becomes a ben Eretz Yisrael immediately.

A ben Eretz Yisrael who travels to Chutz LaAretz with the above intention is considered a ben Chutz LaAretz.[13]

Relocating for the Purpose of Teaching

5. Concerning a ben Eretz Yisrael who travels to Chutz LaAretz with his family[14] to teach for several years; if the school in Chutz LaAretz pays his salary, some authorities deem him a ben Chutz

---

9. *Iggeros Moshe, Orach Chaim*, vol. 3, no. 74. Today, one is not considered to be uprooting his family when he travels to Chutz LaAretz. Therefore, his status is determined by his intention. This is also the view of HaGaon Rav Shlomo Zalman Auerbach, HaGaon Rav Yosef Shalom Eliashiv, HaGaon Rav Shmuel HaLevi Wosner (*Shevet HaLevi*, vol. 5, no. 64), and HaGaon Rav Chaim Pinchus Scheinberg. HaGaon Rav Ben Tziyon Abba Shaul rules likewise for Sephardic couples (see chapter 8 for the Sephardic custom concerning singles).

10. This is based on a ruling by HaGaon Rav Shlomo Zalman Auerbach.

11. *Iggeros Moshe, Orach Chaim*, vol. 3, no. 74. This is also the ruling of HaGaon Rav Chaim Pinchus Scheinberg.

12. This is based on the ruling of HaGaon Rav Yosef Shalom Eliashiv.

13. According to all of the above opinions. See *Iggeros Moshe, Orach Chaim*, vol. 4, no. 109; and *Minchas Yitzchak*, vol. 4, no. 14.

14. If his family remains in Eretz Yisrael, all authorities consider him a ben Eretz Yisrael. If he decides to remain in Chutz LaAretz, however, he is considered a ben Chutz LaAretz even before his family joins him. See *Magen Avraham* 496:7 and *Iggeros Moshe, Orach Chaim*, vol. 4, no. 108.

LaAretz, even if his contract stipulates that he return to Eretz Yisrael after a certain period.[15]

Others rule that he remains a ben Eretz Yisrael.[16] If there is any possibility that he will remain in Chutz LaAretz after his contract expires, all authorities consider him a ben Chutz LaAretz.[17]

One Who is Sent by the Government or His Employer

6. If a ben Eretz Yisrael is sent to Chutz LaAretz by the Israeli government or his employer, and he plans to return to Eretz Yisrael, he is considered a ben Chutz LaAretz according to some authorities[18] and a ben Eretz Yisrael according to others.[19] If there is any possibility that he will remain in Chutz LaAretz, he becomes a ben Chutz LaAretz according to all authorities.[20]

---

15. *Iggeros Moshe, Orach Chaim*, vol. 3, no. 75. Since he may decide to stay longer, he is considered a ben Chutz LaAretz, even though his job is being held for him in Eretz Yisrael. HaGaon Rav Moshe Feinstein's grandson, Rav Mordechai Tendler, wrote the following to a group of Israelis teaching in Chutz LaAretz: "My grandfather explained to me that although we hope you will all return to Eretz Yisrael, during your stay in Chutz LaAretz you are considered b'nei Chutz LaAretz." This is also the ruling of HaGaon Rav Shmuel HaLevi Wosner and HaGaon Rav Ovadia Yossef (*Yechaveh Daas*, vol. 3, no. 35).

HaGaon Rav Yitzchak Yaacov Weiss (*Minchas Yitzchak*, vol. 5, no. 43) advises such people to put on tefillin without the blessing and recite the weekday *Shemoneh Esrei* on Yom Tov Sheini. Yet he agrees that they may not cook for Shabbos on Yom Tov Sheini without making an *eiruv tavshilin*.

16. This is the view of HaGaon Rav Shlomo Zalman Auerbach and HaGaon Rav Yosef Shalom Eliashiv, since he intends to return to Eretz Yisrael and he has limited his stay in Chutz LaAretz. The fact that he brings his family with him is irrelevant in modern times (see note 9).

17. *Minchas Yitzchak*, vol. 4, no. 4.

18. *Chelkas Yaacov*, vol. 3, no. 145; *Minchas Yitzchak*, vol. 4, nos. 1-4; *Yechaveh Daas*, vol. 3, no. 35. This ruling is also indicated in *Iggeros Moshe, Orach Chaim*, vol. 3, no. 75.

19. *Mishneh Halachos* (vol. 4, nos. 83-84) offers three reasons for this ruling: 1) he has limited his stay in Chutz LaAretz; 2) Chazal criticize anyone who gives up a job in Eretz Yisrael to move to Chutz LaAretz; 3) his salary is being paid by his employer in Eretz Yisrael, which obligates him to return. This is also the view of HaGaon Rav Shlomo Zalman Auerbach and HaGaon Rav Yosef Shalom Eliashiv.

20. *Minchas Yitzchak*, vol. 4, no. 4. Also see *Iggeros Moshe, Orach Chaim*, vol. 4, nos. 108-109.

Traveling for Educational Reasons

7. If a ben Eretz Yisrael has been sent to Chutz LaAretz by his employer to take courses related to his profession, and his expenses are paid by his employer with the understanding that he will return to his job when he finishes the courses, he is considered a ben Eretz Yisrael during his stay in Chutz LaAretz, even according to those who rule that a person sent to teach in Chutz LaAretz is considered a ben Chutz LaAretz.[21]

Traveling for Medical Reasons

8. If a ben Eretz Yisrael travels to Chutz LaAretz with his family for more than a year to receive medical attention, but he plans to return afterward, he remains a ben Eretz Yisrael.[22] Some authorities maintain that if he starts a business or takes a steady job, he becomes a ben Chutz LaAretz.[23]

Traveling for One's Wedding

9. A ben Eretz Yisrael who travels to Chutz LaAretz for his wedding but plans to return to Eretz Yisrael to live is considered a ben Eretz Yisrael.[24] His wife remains a bas Chutz LaAretz, however, until she arrives in Eretz Yisrael.[25]

---

21. *Iggeros Moshe, Orach Chaim,* vol. 3, no. 75. Since he has committed himself to returning and his employer is underwriting the trip, we assume that he will honor his commitment. This is also the ruling of HaGaon Rav Shlomo Zalman Auerbach.

22. HaGaon Rav Shlomo Zalman Auerbach explains that since he did not leave Eretz Yisrael to make a living, even if his treatment takes a long time and he needs to find employment in Chutz LaAretz, he remains a ben Eretz Yisrael. This is generally the case if a person is forced to leave Eretz Yisrael but plans to return.

23. *Iggeros Moshe, Orach Chaim,* vol. 4, no. 109.

24. This is based on a ruling by HaGaon Rav Shlomo Zalman Auerbach and HaGaon Rav Yosef Shalom Eliashiv.

25. *Minchas Yitzchak,* vol. 4, no. 3:38. This is also the ruling of HaGaon Rav Shlomo Zalman Auerbach and HaGaon Rav Chaim Pinchus Scheinberg. HaRav Dovid Feinstein and HaRav Elimelech Bluth report that this was the ruling of HaGaon Rav Moshe Feinstein as well.

If he plans on staying in Chutz LaAretz for an extended period after the wedding, he is considered a ben Chutz LaAretz.[26]

10. If a ben Eretz Yisrael travels to Chutz LaAretz for his wedding but plans to return to Eretz Yisrael for three years of study, after which he has promised his in-laws to settle in Chutz LaAretz, he remains a ben Eretz Yisrael while in Chutz LaAretz for his wedding.[27] His wife remains a bas Chutz LaAretz until she arrives in Eretz Yisrael, whereupon she becomes a bas Eretz Yisrael despite their commitment to return to Chutz LaAretz.[28] Only when they

---

HaGaon Rav Auerbach adds that although a woman normally adopts her husband's customs, Yom Tov Sheini is different since it is a universally accepted practice. See note 28. HaGaon Rav Auerbach further notes that her husband may put on tefillin in her presence without denigrating Yom Tov since she knows that he is a ben Eretz Yisrael. See chapter 4, note 16.

26. *Iggeros Moshe, Orach Chaim*, vol. 3, no. 75. Since he may be forced to delay his return until he becomes more settled financially, his in-laws may find him a job and insist that he live nearby. He must therefore consider himself a ben Chutz LaAretz until he returns to Eretz Yisrael.

However, it is unclear at what point such a visit becomes problematic. The reasoning of *Iggeros Moshe* implies that even a short-term visit would render him a ben Chutz LaAretz; but the case in point was a period of nearly two years. This period is also mentioned in *Iggeros Moshe, Orach Chaim*, vol. 4, no. 108. According to HaRav Dovid Feinstein, his father applied this ruling whenever a couple was to remain in Chutz LaAretz long enough to need to consider a livelihood. But if they have no intention of working, even if they stay for several months, the husband remains a ben Eretz Yisrael.

BeTzeil HaChochmah (vol. 1, no. 64) rules that if he owns an apartment in Eretz Yisrael and has left all his possessions there, he remains a ben Eretz Yisrael. HaGaon Rav Shlomo Zalman Auerbach reasons that newlyweds generally remain in town for a short time after the wedding. But if they rent an apartment for six months or longer, this is no longer considered a visit and the groom becomes a ben Chutz LaAretz.

27. This is based on a ruling by HaGaon Rav Shlomo Zalman Auerbach. Although he has committed himself to settling in Chutz LaAretz eventually, he presumably wishes to remain in Eretz Yisrael. Since after three years his in-laws may allow them to stay, he remains a ben Eretz Yisrael.

28. This is based on a ruling by HaGaon Rav Shlomo Zalman Auerbach. Although she plans on returning to Chutz LaAretz three years later, once she arrives in Eretz Yisrael she adopts all her husband's customs (unlike the situation described in note 25, where she has not yet left Chutz LaAretz).

actually move to Chutz LaAretz do they both become b'nei Chutz LaAretz.

A Bar Mitzvah in Eretz Yisrael

11. A ben Chutz LaAretz who becomes bar mitzvah in Eretz Yisrael remains a resident of Chutz LaAretz.[29]

Conversion to Judaism

12. Some authorities rule that one who converts to Judaism while visiting Eretz Yisrael is considered a ben Chutz LaAretz with respect to Yom Tov Sheini.[30] Others maintain that he becomes a ben Eretz Yisrael until he returns to his country of origin to live.[31]

---

29. This is the ruling of HaGaon Rav Shlomo Zalman Auerbach (*Minchas Shlomo*, no. 19) and HaGaon Rav Yosef Shalom Eliashiv, although he becomes obligated in mitzvos while in Eretz Yisrael. *BeTzeil HaChochmah* (vol. 1, no. 77), however, disagrees. Also see *Shaarei Yitzchak*, no. 4, note 14.

30. HaGaon Rav Shlomo Zalman Auerbach, *Minchas Shlomo*, no. 19.

31. *BeTzeil HaChochmah*, vol. 1, no. 36. This is also the ruling of HaGaon Rav Yosef Shalom Eliashiv, since the person may decide to remain in Eretz Yisrael and he was not obligated to observe Yom Tov in Chutz LaAretz. This is not comparable to the case of a child visiting Eretz Yisrael for his bar mitzvah (paragraph 11): since he is dependent on his parents, their intention to return to Chutz LaAretz obligates him as well.

CHAPTER 7
Dual Residency

One Who Spends Equal Time in
Eretz Yisrael and Chutz LaAretz

1. If one spends half the year in Eretz Yisrael and half in Chutz LaAretz, and earns a livelihood in both places, he observes one day of Yom Tov in Eretz Yisrael and two days in Chutz LaAretz.[1] If his income comes from only one of the two places, some authorities consider him a resident of that place.[2]

One Who Spends Most of the Year in One Place

2. A person who spends most of the year in one place is con-

---

1. *Maharit Tzahlon*, no. 52 (concerning one who spends every other year in Eretz Yisrael); HaGaon Rav Y. Z. Mintzberg in *Noam*, vol. 2, p. 70; *Minchas Yitzchak*, vol. 4, no. 4, footnote; and *BeTzeil HaChochmah*, vol. 4, no. 126. HaGaon Rav Shlomo Zalman Auerbach adds it is sufficient to spend approximately the same amount of time in each place. HaGaon Rav Ben Tziyon Abba Shaul relates that this is also the Sephardic custom. If one owns an apartment in only one place, however, see note 4.

HaGaon Rav Yosef Shalom Eliashiv, however, considers his status questionable and rules that in Eretz Yisrael he should not perform *melachah* on Yom Tov Sheini or eat *chametz* on the eighth day of Pesach.

2. This is the ruling of HaGaon Rav Yosef Shalom Eliashiv.

sidered a resident of that place, even for those holidays he spends in the other place,[3] and even if he owns a home only in the place where he spends less time.[4]

3. If one's family lives in Eretz Yisrael but his job takes him to Chutz LaAretz most of the year, he is considered is a ben Eretz Yisrael.[5]

A Ben Chutz LaAretz Who Spends Every Yom Tov in Eretz Yisrael

4. Some authorities rule that a ben Chutz LaAretz who spends every Yom Tov[6] in Eretz Yisrael is considered a ben Eretz Yisrael.[7] If he is forced to spend one Yom Tov in Chutz LaAretz, however, he

---

3. This is the view of HaGaon Rav Y. Z. Mintzberg, HaGaon Rav Shlomo Zalman Auerbach, and HaGaon Rav Yosef Shalom Eliashiv. Also see HaGaon Rav Shmuel HaLevi Wosner, *Shevet HaLevi*, vol. 5, no. 64.

4. *Iggeros Moshe* (*Orach Chaim*, vol. 3, no. 74) explains that nowadays ownership of a home does not establish residence; many people purchase homes in Eretz Yisrael with no intention of settling there. HaGaon Rav Shlomo Zalman Auerbach and HaGaon Rav Yosef Shalom Eliashiv agree.

Nevertheless, HaGaon Rav Chaim Pinchus Scheinberg rules that residence is determined by the location of one's home, even if he does not live there most of the year. But this only applies if he bought the home in order to live in it—not as an investment. I have heard from HaGaon Rav Ben Tziyon Abba Shaul that this is the Sephardic custom.

5. HaGaon Rav Yosef Shalom Eliashiv explains that spending most of the year in Chutz LaAretz does not change one's status unless his stay is of a permanent nature.

6. Including Shavuos, contrary to popular misconception.

7. HaGaon Rav Shlomo Zalman Auerbach explains that the enactment of Yom Tov Sheini only applies to b'nei Chutz LaAretz who would have had to observe two days regularly had they lived in the period when Rosh Chodesh was determined by the sighting of the new moon. Since a person who spends every Yom Tov in Eretz Yisrael would have been exempt from observing Yom Tov Sheini in those days, he is exempt today as well. HaGaon Rav Auerbach's ruling is discussed in detail in *Minchas Shlomo*, no. 19:7. There he concludes that one who wishes to act stringently should only refrain from *melachah*; he should not recite Kiddush or the Yom Tov *Shemoneh Esrei* and should wear tefillin if it is not Chol HaMoed.

observes Yom Tov Sheini. Yet most authorities consider him a ben Chutz LaAretz even for those Yamim Tovim that he spends in Eretz Yisrael.[8]

A resident of Eretz Yisrael who spends every Yom Tov in Chutz LaAretz remains a ben Eretz Yisrael.[9]

Although the actual responsa in *Minchas Shlomo* refers to a person who owns a home in Eretz Yisrael, HaGaon Rav Auerbach has told me that the same ruling would apply to a person who spends every Yom Tov in Eretz Yisrael in a hotel or a rented apartment.

8. This is the view of HaGaon Rav Yosef Shalom Eliashiv and most contemporary authorities, who maintain that the enactment of Yom Tov Sheini applies to any resident of Chutz LaAretz, regardless of what his status would have been in ancient times.

9. The enactment of Yom Tov Sheini only applies to people who permanently reside in Chutz LaAretz.

CHAPTER 8
Laws Pertaining
to a Single Person

A Ben Chutz LaAretz Who Comes to Eretz Yisrael

1. An unmarried ben Chutz LaAretz[1] who goes to Eretz Yisrael
for a short time, intending to return to Chutz LaAretz, remains a
ben Chutz LaAretz.[2] But if he settles in Eretz Yisrael and is financially independent, he becomes a ben Eretz Yisrael immediately, as
explained in chapter five.

Torah Study

2. Early authorities debate the status of an unmarried, financially
independent ben Chutz LaAretz who goes to Eretz Yisrael to study
Torah for an extended period.[3] Among Ashkenazim, such a person

---

1. This chapter applies equally to men and women. Concerning Sephardic communities, see paragraph 5.

2. *Shaarei Teshuvah* 496:2; *Mishnah Berurah* 496:13. But see note 3.

3. *Chaim She'al* (no. 55) cites an ancient debate between the rabbis of Safed and
Jerusalem, the former ruling that such a person observes Yom Tov Sheini, and the
latter maintaining that since he may find a wife in Eretz Yisrael and remain there, he

observes Yom Tov Sheini.[4] Some Sephardic authorities rule that he observes one day of Yom Tov. Others limit this ruling to specific situations.[5]

3. If the student accepts his parents' decisions and they prefer that he return to Chutz LaAretz, some authorities consider him a ben Chutz LaAretz, whether he is Ashkenazic[6] or Sephardic.[7]

---

is considered a ben Eretz Yisrael. *Chaim She'al* sides with the rabbis of Jerusalem. This is also the conclusion of *Shaarei Teshuvah, Shalmei Chagigah,* and *Shevus Yaacov* (no. 79). Nevertheless, *She'eilas Yaavetz* (no. 168) and *Ginas Veradim* (vol. 1, no. 14) follow the rabbis of Safed. Also see *Minchas Yitzchak,* vol. 4, no. 4; *Yabia Omer,* vol. 6, no. 40; and *Shaarei Yitzchak* 7:1.

4. *Maharam Shick,* no. 248, based on the Rema, *Orach Chaim* 468:17. This is also the ruling of *Iggeros Moshe, Orach Chaim,* vol. 2, no. 101; *Chelkas Yaacov,* vol. 3, no. 154; and HaGaon Rav Shlomo Zalman Auerbach, HaGaon Rav Yosef Shalom Eliashiv, and HaGaon Rav Chaim Pinchus Scheinberg.

5. This is the ruling of HaGaon Rav Ben Tziyon Abba Shaul, who adds that many Sephardic authorities follow the Chacham Tzvi, who states that a person's status regarding Yom Tov Sheini depends on where he is, not where he is from.
Other Sephardic authorities rule that he observes two days unless he would consider marrying an Israeli and settling in Eretz Yisrael and his parents would not object. I have heard this ruling from several Sephardic *roshei yeshiva* in Yerushalayim and B'nei Brak. It is also implied in *Yabia Omer,* vol. 6, no. 40.

6. According to HaGaon Rav Moshe Feinstein (*Iggeros Moshe,* vol. 2, no. 101), only students who are financially independent or whose parents support their plans to settle in Eretz Yisrael may observe one day of Yom Tov. HaGaon Rav Shlomo Zalman Auerbach notes that although many students may say they have decided to settle in Eretz Yisrael, such statements do not affect their halachic status since most of them will not defy their parents. One's status only changes if he is resolved to settle in Eretz Yisrael, despite parental objections. But if one's parents have explicitly endorsed his decision to remain in Eretz Yisrael, and will continue to support him, he becomes a ben Eretz Yisrael even though he accepts his parents' decisions.
In contrast: "The Chazon Ish ruled [that such a student] should refrain from *melachah* [on Yom Tov Sheini], but should put on tefillin and recite the weekday *Shemoneh Esrei.* The Gaon of Tchebin maintained that he observes all the laws of Yom Tov Sheini. I am told that this was also the ruling of HaGaon Rav Yosef Tzvi Dushinsky. Our master, HaGaon Rav Yitzchak Zev Soloveitchik of Brisk, leaned toward the view of the Chazon Ish but never reached a definitive decision. HaGaon Rav Reuven Bengis, employing [in this doubtful situation] the opinion of the Chacham Tzvi, ruled that he should observe one day of Yom Tov" (*Moadim U'Zemanim,* vol. 7, no. 120).

Tefillin

4. Most authorities concur that one should not lay tefillin on Yom Tov Sheini in Eretz Yisrael, and this is the accepted custom.[8]

A Student Who is Engaged

5. If a ben Chutz LaAretz is engaged to a girl in Chutz LaAretz and goes to study in Eretz Yisrael until his wedding, he observes Yom Tov Sheini. This applies to Sephardim as well.[9]

6. A ben Chutz LaAretz who became engaged to a girl in Eretz Yisrael and plans on settling there is considered a ben Eretz Yisrael, even if he spends a Yom Tov in Chutz LaAretz before his wedding.

---

7. HaGaon Rav Ben Tziyon Abba Shaul adds that a seventeen-year-old boy and a sixteen-year-old girl are considered independent, but other authorities do not consider age a factor.

Because many factors determine "independence," a halachic authority must be consulted in all questionable situations.

8. *Iggeros Moshe, Orach Chaim,* vol. 2, no. 101; and *Chelkas Yaacov,* vol. 3, no. 153. Since nowadays many people question the observance of Yom Tov Sheini, one must not give them any excuse to take it lightly. Even putting on tefillin privately may result in a degradation of Yom Tov. See *Kesav Sofer, Orach Chaim,* no. 10. *Shaarei Yitzchak* reports that originally the Gaon of Tchebin instructed visiting students to put on tefillin without reciting the blessing, but after becoming aware of the movement (especially among Reform Jews) to eliminate Yom Tov Sheini, he forbade students to wear them.

HaGaon Rav Shlomo Zalman Auerbach, however, rules that a *ben Torah* who might settle in Eretz Yisrael should put on tefillin on Yom Tov Sheini (if it is not Chol HaMoed in Eretz Yisrael) without a blessing. He notes that since many rabbis of Yerushalayim—including HaGaon Rav Shmuel Salant—took the Chacham Tzvi's view into account in resolving questions relating to Yom Tov Sheini, a *ben Torah* should put on tefillin on Yom Tov Sheini because it is a Torah obligation. He should also mentally stipulate that if the law bears out the opinion of the Chacham Tzvi, he is wearing the tefillin for the sake of the mitzvah; and if not, they should be considered a regular garment. But only one who is generally very conscientious about performing mitzvos should act this way, since he will not come to neglect the observance of Yom Tov Sheini in any way.

9. See *Kaf HaChaim, Orach Chaim* 468:45, in the name of *Mizbach Adamah*; and *Shaarei Yitzchak* 7:5.

If the wedding will take place in Chutz LaAretz, some authorities rule that he remains a ben Chutz LaAretz,[10] while others consider him a ben Eretz Yisrael.[11]

An Extended Stay

7.   If an unmarried ben Chutz LaAretz goes to Eretz Yisrael for an indefinite period, intending to remain there if he finds employment, some authorities consider him a ben Eretz Yisrael.[12]

---

10. *Iggeros Moshe* (*Orach Chaim*, vol. 4, no. 108) rules that he remains dependent on his parents, even in Eretz Yisrael.

11. This is based on a ruling by HaGaon Rav Shlomo Zalman Auerbach and *Shaarei Yitzchak* 7:5. Once he becomes engaged and decides to settle in Eretz Yisrael, he is no longer dependent on his parents to the extent that their objections will cause him to alter his plans.

12. This is based on a ruling by HaGaon Rav Shlomo Zalman Auerbach. Based on *Iggeros Moshe, Orach Chaim*, vol. 2, no. 101 (see note 6), it is unclear whether HaGaon Rav Moshe Feinstein would agree, or whether he felt that such a person should observe Yom Tov Sheini until he is resolved to settle in Eretz Yisrael.

CHAPTER 9
Kiddush, Havdalah, and Candlelighting

Kiddush

1. A ben Eretz Yisrael may not recite Kiddush for a ben Chutz LaAretz on Yom Tov Sheini, whether in Eretz Yisrael[1] or in Chutz

---

1. This issue is debated among the early authorities. *Ginas Veradim* (*Orach Chaim*, no. 1:13) cites Rav Moshe ben Chaviv, who rules that a ben Eretz Yisrael may recite the Yom Tov prayers on behalf of a ben Chutz LaAretz on Yom Tov Sheini, for although a person who is not obligated in a mitzvah may not perform that mitzvah on behalf of someone who is (*Rosh HaShanah* 29a), this rule only applies where the person performing the mitzvah has no obligation at all. For example, since a woman is not obligated in the time-bound mitzvah of *shofar*, she cannot blow the *shofar* to discharge a man of his obligation. But since a resident of a large city is obligated to read the Megillah on the fourteenth of Adar, he could have read it on behalf of a villager, who read the Megillah on the Monday or Thursday prior to Purim in Talmudic times (Rashi, *Megillah* 2a).

Nevertheless, *Ginas Veradim* rules that only someone with the same obligation as someone else may perform a mitzvah on his behalf. This is also the conclusion of R. Akiva Eiger in his glosses on *Shulchan Aruch* 496:3 and 690:10.

LaAretz.[2] If he did so in Chutz LaAretz, he has fulfilled his obligation,[3] but in Eretz Yisrael the ben Chutz LaAretz must repeat Kiddush.[4]

2. If a ben Eretz Yisrael is married to a bas Chutz LaAretz (see chapter 6, paragraph 9), he may not recite Kiddush for her on the night of Yom Tov Sheini, even if the local residents are aware that he is not doing so.[5] Either a ben Chutz LaAretz should recite Kiddush for her or she should do so herself.[6]

3. A ben Eretz Yisrael may recite Kiddush for a ben Chutz LaAretz on Shabbos morning when Yom Tov Sheini falls on Shabbos. But he must intend to discharge the listener of his obligation to recite Kiddush for both Shabbos and Yom Tov.[7]

---

2. *Imrei Binah* (*Hilchos Shabbos*, no. 11) asserts that in Chutz LaAretz the ben Eretz Yisrael could theoretically become obligated in the mitzvah of Kiddush by deciding to remain there; therefore, he may recite Kiddush on behalf of a ben Chutz LaAretz. But R. Akiva Eiger (in his glosses on *Shulchan Aruch* 267) questions this logic, and *BeTzeil HaChochmah* (vol. 1, no. 55) rejects it. HaGaon Rav Shlomo Zalman Auerbach and HaGaon Rav Yosef Shalom Eliashiv conclude that one should not rely on the Imrei Binah in this matter.

3. See note 2. Once Kiddush has been recited for the ben Chutz LaAretz, he should not repeat it, for he has fulfilled his obligation according to the Imrei Binah.

4. *BeTzeil HaChochmah*, vol. 1, no. 55. The Imrei Binah's logic only applies in Chutz LaAretz, and since all later authorities reject the view of Rav Moshe ben Chaviv (cited in note 1), his view cannot be relied upon, even after the fact.

5. This is based on a ruling by HaGaon Rav Shlomo Zalman Auerbach.

6. HaGaon Rav Yosef Shalom Eliashiv rules that a woman should recite Kiddush herself rather than rely on the view of the Imrei Binah.

7. This is based on a ruling by HaGaon Rav Shlomo Zalman Auerbach. The mitzvah of Kiddush in the morning is fulfilled by reciting the blessing of *Borei pri hagafen* over a cup of wine—the practice of reciting verses from the Torah in honor of the day is purely customary; thus, a ben Eretz Yisrael and a ben Chutz LaAretz are both obligated in the same type of Kiddush.

Havdalah

4. On the night of Yom Tov Sheini, a ben Eretz Yisrael in Chutz LaAretz inserts "*Atah Chonantanu*" in *maariv*.[8] Some authorities rule that he should not recite Havdalah.[9] Most, however, maintain that he should do so privately,[10] and if he forgets that night, he should recite it the following day.[11] But if he also forgets that day, he should fulfill the mitzvah by listening to the recitation of a ben Chutz LaAretz.[12]

5. If Yom Tov Sheini begins Saturday night, a ben Eretz Yisrael visiting Chutz LaAretz (and following the view in paragraph 4 requiring him to recite Havdalah) should not kindle a candle in order to recite the blessing over fire.[13] Rather, he should connect two Yom Tov candles, recite the blessing, and then leave them burning.[14] If there are no other candles burning, some authorities

---

8. HaGaon Rav Moshe Feinstein, *Iggeros Moshe, Orach Chaim*, vol. 3, no. 72.

9. *She'eilas Yaavetz* (no. 168) maintains that since he is forbidden to perform *melachah*, he should not recite Havdalah. *Iggeros Moshe* (*Orach Chaim*, vol. 3, no. 72) rules likewise without explanation. HaRav Shmuel Feurst, a student of HaGaon Rav Moshe Feinstein, reports that he compared Havdalah to *melachah*, which is forbidden even in private (see chapter 4, paragraph 1).

10. *BeTzeil HaChochmah* (vol. 1, no. 22) cites many authorities who rule that Havdalah, like prayer, does not lead to a degradation of Yom Tov Sheini when recited privately. This is also the view of HaGaon Rav Shlomo Zalman Auerbach, HaGaon Rav Yosef Shalom Eliashiv, and HaGaon Rav Shmuel HaLevi Wosner.

11. A person who did not recite Havdalah on *motza'ei Shabbos* may do so anytime before Tuesday night. Although most authorities rule that there is no such compensation for Havdalah after Yom Tov, R. Akiva Eiger (in his novellae on *Pesachim* 117a) states that since the day follows the night in Jewish law, the next day is still "*motza'ei Yom Tov*," so reciting Havdalah then is not considered "compensation." Also see *BeTzeil HaChochmah*, vol. 1, no. 23; *Sdeh Chemed, Asifas Dinim, Maareches HaAlef*, par. 15; and *Pischei Aravim* on *Arvei Pesachim* (Fried), chap. 28.

12. Ibid. Some authorities rule that one may compensate for Havdalah for three days after Yom Tov. To take this view into account, he should listen to another's recitation.

13. *BeTzeil HaChochmah*, vol. 1, no. 22:5.

14. See chapter 1, paragraph 14.

permit him to strike a match,[15] but others forbid it.[16]

6. If a ben Eretz Yisrael is married to a bas Chutz LaAretz (see chapter 6, paragraph 9), he should ask someone to recite Havdalah for her after Yom Tov Sheini.[17] If he cannot find anyone to do so, she should recite it herself.[18]

7. A ben Eretz Yisrael who mistakenly said *"Atah Chonantanu"* on *motza'ei Yom Tov Sheini* need not repeat *Shemoneh Esrei.*[19]

When Yom Tov Sheini Falls on Shabbos

8. A ben Chutz LaAretz may light the Shabbos candles and recite the blessing for a ben Eretz Yisrael, even though he includes both Shabbos and Yom Tov in his blessing.[20]

9. A ben Eretz Yisrael should not light Shabbos candles for a ben Chutz LaAretz. If he did so, bearing in mind that he was lighting

---

15. This is based on a ruling by HaGaon Rav Shlomo Zalman Auerbach and HaGaon Rav Shmuel HaLevi Wosner. HaGaon Rav Auerbach adds that if he cannot find a private place to light a match, the blessing may be recited over a light bulb. (See HaGaon Rav Auerbach's *Me'orei Eish*, p. 93, regarding the permissibility of reciting the blessing in this manner.)

16. This is the view of HaGaon Rav Yosef Shalom Eliashiv, for whom it makes no difference whether *melachah* was done for a mitzvah or for other purposes. According to HaGaon Rav Moshe Feinstein, who prohibits the recitation of Havdalah because it is considered a public act (see note 9), it would certainly be forbidden to strike a match for the blessing.

17. This is based on a ruling by HaGaon Rav Shlomo Zalman Auerbach and HaGaon Rav Yosef Shalom Eliashiv. According to *Shaarei Yitzchak* (9:4), the husband should ask in such a way that it not appear obvious that he only observes one day of Yom Tov. But as explained above (chapter 4, note 14), one need not be concerned with dissent *after* Yom Tov, and may ask in a normal fashion.

18. This is the ruling of HaGaon Rav Yosef Shalom Eliashiv, based on *Mishnah Berurah* 296:35 and *Shaar HaTziyun* 296:34. Although it is preferable for a woman to hear Havdalah recited by a man, if she cannot find one she should recite it herself.

19. *BeTzeil HaChochmah*, vol. 1, no. 22:3.

20. This is based on a ruling by HaGaon Rav Shlomo Zalman Auerbach. Although the ben Eretz Yisrael need only mention Shabbos in his blessing, the words "Yom Tov" are not considered an interruption.

both Shabbos and Yom Tov candles on his behalf, the ben Chutz LaAretz has fulfilled his obligation.[21] If he only intended the candles to be for Shabbos, not Yom Tov, and the ben Chutz LaAretz did not yet accept Shabbos, he should light Yom Tov candles himself, but the blessing should be omitted.

10. A ben Eretz Yisrael in Chutz LaAretz should listen to his host recite Kiddush rather than reciting it himself.[22] If he can recite the Shabbos Kiddush discreetly, however, he may do so.[23]

11. A ben Chutz LaAretz in Eretz Yisrael must recite Kiddush himself. If there is only one cup of wine, some authorities rule that the host should recite Kiddush over wine and the guest over bread,[24] while others maintain that the guest should recite the Yom Tov Kiddush over wine for himself and his host.[25]

12. A ben Eretz Yisrael may recite Havdalah for a ben Chutz LaAretz.[26]

---

21. HaGaon Rav Shlomo Zalman Auerbach explains that Yom Tov is also called "Shabbos." Therefore, the ben Chutz LaAretz has fulfilled his obligation although the ben Eretz Yisrael did not mention Yom Tov.

22. Since his host mentions Shabbos in the Yom Tov Kiddush, a ben Eretz Yisrael can fulfill his obligation with this recitation. See *Birkei Yosef* 213:1, in the name of *Leket HaKemach*; and *Be'er Moshe*, p. 116. *BeTzeil HaChochmah* (vol. 1, no. 26) deduces from *Birkei Yosef* that this is preferable to reciting the Friday night Kiddush, which may lead to a degradation of Yom Tov. I have heard a similar ruling from HaGaon Rav Yosef Shalom Eliashiv. HaRav Shmuel Feurst writes that this was also the ruling of HaGaon Rav Moshe Feinstein. Also see *Har Tzvi, Orach Chaim*, vol. 1, no. 154; and *Iggeros Moshe, Orach Chaim*, vol. 4, nos. 21:9 and 101:1.

If he eats alone, he recites the regular Friday night Kiddush.

23. *Be'er Moshe*, p. 116. HaRav Shmuel Feurst has also informed me that this was how HaGaon Rav Moshe Feinstein ruled.

24. *BeTzeil HaChochmah*, vol. 1, no. 26. Clearly, if the host agrees, he may recite Kiddush over bread and have his guest recite it over wine.

25. This is based on a ruling by HaGaon Rav Yosef Shalom Eliashiv. See note 22.

26. So rules HaGaon Rav Shlomo Zalman Auerbach, since they are both obligated to recite the same Havdalah. This was also reportedly the view of the Steipler Gaon, Rav Y. Y. Kanievsky. Also see *Shevet HaKehasi*, vol. 1, no. 155.

Nevertheless, according to HaGaon Rav Moshe Soloveitchik of Zurich, the Chazon Ish felt that a ben Chutz LaAretz probably cannot fulfill his obligation by listening to a ben Eretz Yisrael.

CHAPTER 10
Tefillah BeTzibbur

Forming a Minyan

1. It is customary for people visiting Eretz Yisrael to form a Yom Tov Sheini minyan. They may read the Torah and the haftorah and recite all the Yom Tov prayers.[1]

2. Some authorities rule that groups of fewer than ten b'nei Chutz LaAretz should daven in private rather than asking b'nei Eretz Yisrael to complete their minyan.[2] Others allow b'nei Eretz Yisrael to help them form a minyan for kerias haTorah—if the Torah is read that day in Eretz Yisrael as well—but not in order to repeat the Yom Tov Shemoneh Esrei.[3] Still other authorities allow

---

1. Residents of Eretz Yisrael may not form a weekday minyan on Yom Tov Sheini in Chutz LaAretz. See chapter 3, note 6.

2. This is the view of HaGaon Rav Shlomo Zalman Auerbach. Although b'nei Chutz LaAretz customarily form their own minyanim today, since many rabbis in previous generations opposed this practice, b'nei Eretz Yisrael should not participate. Also see Halachos Ketanos, vol. 1, no. 4; Kaf HaChaim, Orach Chaim 496:39; and Be'er Moshe, p. 190.

3. Har Tzvi, Orach Chaim, no. 70, based on Pri Megadim 566.

b'nei Eretz Yisrael to complete a minyan for b'nei Chutz LaAretz in all cases.[4]

3. Some authorities rule that visitors from Eretz Yisrael may help form a minyan on Yom Tov Sheini in Chutz LaAretz,[5] whereupon all the Yom Tov prayers and Torah readings may be recited.[6] Others only allow them to help form a minyan for the Torah reading—if the Torah is read that day in Eretz Yisrael as well—but not for reciting *mussaf* or repeating the Yom Tov *Shemoneh Esrei*.[7]

Zimun

4. B'nei Chutz LaAretz and b'nei Eretz Yisrael may form a *zimun* together on Yom Tov Sheini.[8]

Receiving an *Aliyah*

In Chutz LaAretz

5. A ben Eretz Yisrael should not be called up to the Torah on the eighth day of Pesach, the second day of Shavuos, and Simchas Torah.[9]

---

4. *Kaf HaChaim, Orach Chaim* 496:39, citing other authorities; *BeTzeil HaChochmah*, vol. 1, no. 3:3; *Shaarei Yitzchak* 11:3. HaGaon Rav Yosef Shalom Eliashiv rules that four b'nei Eretz Yisrael can even combine with six b'nei Chutz LaAretz.

5. HaGaon Rav Moshe Feinstein, *Iggeros Moshe, Orach Chaim*, vol. 4, no. 106.

6. Ibid. If b'nei Eretz Yisrael were forbidden to complete the minyan, it would become obvious that they are not observing Yom Tov, which would lead to a degradation of the day.

7. This is based on a ruling by HaGaon Rav Shlomo Zalman Auerbach.

8. Although the b'nei Chutz LaAretz recite *Yaaleh VeYavo* in their *birkas hamazon* and the b'nei Eretz Yisrael do not, HaGaon Rav Shlomo Zalman Auerbach has ruled that because the main obligation—thanking HaShem for their meal—is the same for both, they may combine to form a *zimun*.

9. *Shaarei Teshuvah* 496:5. Since it is a weekday for him, the blessings over the Torah are being recited in vain. On the other hand, *Shevus Yaacov* (no. 40) allows him to receive an *aliyah* since he may decide to remain in Chutz LaAretz and become obligated to read the Torah that day. *Shaarei Ephraim* (8:97) concludes that it is preferable not to call a ben Eretz Yisrael to the Torah.

If he was nonetheless called up, he should pretend to be in the middle of the Shema or *Shemoneh Esrei*.[10] But if it is obvious that he is refusing the *aliyah* because he is not observing Yom Tov, he should accept it and recite the blessings, even if the Torah is not read that day in Eretz Yisrael.[11]

If the eighth day of Pesach or second day of Shavuos falls on Shabbos, some authorities permit a ben Eretz Yisrael to be given an *aliyah*,[12] but others are doubtful.[13]

On Simchas Torah, a ben Eretz Yisrael may be given the *aliyah* of *chasan Torah* (the reading of the final verses of the Torah) if he is a *talmid chacham*.[14] Otherwise, even a wealthy ben Eretz Yisrael should not be given this honor.[15]

---

10. *Shaarei Ephraim* 8:97. I have also heard this ruling from HaGaon Rav Shlomo Zalman Auerbach.

11. This is based on a ruling by HaGaon Rav Shlomo Zalman Auerbach. Publicizing his non-observance of Yom Tov would lead to a public degradation of the sanctity of the day. Furthermore, his blessings over the Torah are not said in vain because they were enacted in honor of the congregation—not to fulfill an individual obligation. This ruling can also be inferred from *Magen Avraham* 566:8 and *Mishnah Berurah* 566:19. Also see *Iggeros Moshe, Yoreh Deah*, vol. 3, no. 96:8.

12. *BeTzeil HaChochmah* 1:3. HaRav Shmuel Feurst writes that HaGaon Rav Moshe Feinstein ruled that a ben Eretz Yisrael can fulfill his obligation to hear the reading of the Torah on Shabbos by listening to the Yom Tov reading; the basic requirement is fulfilled by listening to seven people being called to the Torah—the practice of completing the Torah every year by reading a specific *sidrah* each week is purely customary.

13. HaGaon Rav Shlomo Zalman Auerbach explains that since he is obligated to hear the weekly *sidrah*, it may be improper to call him up for the Torah reading of Yom Tov.

14. HaGaon Rav Shlomo Zalman Auerbach agrees in this case (see note 15), since *chasan Torah* is not one of the regular *aliyos* and is only added in honor of the completion of the Torah, and calling up the *talmid chacham* does honor to the Torah. HaRav Shmuel Feurst writes that HaGaon Rav Moshe Feinstein concurred.

15. This is based on a ruling by HaGaon Rav Shlomo Zalman Auerbach. Although the Rema (*Orach Chaim* 282:3) rules that calling up a wealthy person for *chasan Torah* shows respect for the Torah, since a ben Eretz Yisrael does not observe Yom Tov that day, it is improper.

6. On the second day of Pesach and Sukkos—when the Torah readings in Eretz Yisrael and Chutz LaAretz are identical—a ben Eretz Yisrael may accept an *aliyah*[16] (as may a ben Chutz LaAretz in Eretz Yisrael).[17] However, if he is given *maftir*, some authorities rule that a ben Chutz LaAretz should recite the haftorah and its blessings.[18]

7. During Chol HaMoed Sukkos, a ben Eretz Yisrael may receive the second or fourth *aliyah*, but not the first or third, which differ from those read in Eretz Yisrael.[19]

In Eretz Yisrael

8. Some authorities rule that on Yom Tov Sheini a ben Chutz LaAretz fulfills the mitzvah of davening with a congregation even if he attends a weekday minyan, even though he recites the Yom Tov Shemoneh Esrei.[20]

9. If Yom Tov Sheini falls on Shabbos, a ben Chutz LaAretz may be called up to the Torah in a minyan of b'nei Eretz Yisrael, even though he is not obligated to hear the weekly Torah reading,[21] and even if he has already heard the Yom Tov reading elsewhere.[22] But he should

---

16. *Shaarei Ephraim* 8:97.

17. This is based on a ruling by HaGaon Rav Shlomo Zalman Auerbach.

18. Ibid. This ruling appears difficult, since a public degradation of Yom Tov may result. Indeed, HaGaon Rav Shlomo Zalman Auerbach writes that a ben Eretz Yisrael should not be called up for *maftir* for this reason. We have thus cited this ruling in the name of "some authorities."

19. Ibid.

20. This is the ruling of HaGaon Rav Shlomo Zalman Auerbach and HaGaon Rav Yosef Shalom Eliashiv, but *Chelkas Yaacov* (no. 146) disagrees.

21. This is based on a ruling by HaGaon Rav Shlomo Zalman Auerbach and *BeTzeil HaChochmah*, vol. 1, no. 8, and vol. 3, nos. 1-2. Also see *Luach Eretz Yisrael*; the Shabbos volume of *Yesodei Yeshurun*, p. 428; and *Shaarei Yitzchak* 11:7.

22. In support of this ruling, HaGaon Rav Shlomo Zalman Auerbach cites *Mishnah Berurah* 282:32: one who has been called to the Torah in one synagogue may receive an *aliyah* in another. Nevertheless, *Shaarei Yitzchak* (11:7) cites *Mishneh Sachir* (no. 90), which rules stringently.

not be called up for *maftir*. If he was nonetheless, he should conclude the blessings following the haftorah with the words "*Mekadesh
haShabbos*," without adding "*vehazemanim*."[23]

10. On Simchas Torah (Shemini Atzeres in Chutz LaAretz), a ben
Chutz LaAretz may be honored with the *aliyah* of *chasan Torah*.[24]

A ben Chutz LaAretz may receive an *aliyah* on Chol HaMoed
Sukkos—even on the first day (Yom Tov Sheini in Chutz LaAretz),[25]
although the reading begins with the words "And on the second
day...."[26]

11. When Simchas Torah falls on Shabbos, he may be called to the
Torah at *minchah*, even though the congregation reads from *Bereishis*
whereas in Chutz LaAretz they read from *VeZos HaBrachah*.[27]

Serving as a *Sheliach Tzibbur*

12. A ben Eretz Yisrael may not function as a *sheliach tzibbur* on Yom
Tov Sheini in Chutz LaAretz. Similarly, a ben Chutz LaAretz may not
be the *sheliach tzibbur* for a weekday minyan in Eretz Yisrael.[28]

13. A ben Chutz LaAretz may serve as the *sheliach tzibbur* for
mussaf on Chol HaMoed Sukkos in a minyan of b'nei Eretz Yisrael.
In his silent *Shemoneh Esrei*, he should say the verses recited in
Chutz LaAretz. But when repeating the *Shemoneh Esrei*, he should
follow the custom of Eretz Yisrael. The converse is true of a ben

---

23. This is based on a ruling by HaGaon Rav Shlomo Zalman Auerbach. Since the
blessings over the haftorah were enacted for the congregation, he recites them
according to the practice of the congregation in which he prays.

24. *Kaf HaChaim, Orach Chaim* 496:61, citing the consensus of the rabbis of Yerushalayim; and *Luach Eretz Yisrael*.

25. This is based on a ruling by HaGaon Rav Shlomo Zalman Auerbach.

26. Ibid. In Chutz LaAretz, the sacrifices brought on both that day of Chol HaMoed and
the previous day are mentioned because of the doubt as to which day of Sukkos it
actually is. In Eretz Yisrael, only the sacrifice for that day is mentioned.

27. *Shaarei Yitzchak* 11:8, based on *BeTzeil HaChochmah*, vol. 1, nos. 3:10 and 5:7.

28. Ibid. See chapter 11, paragraph 6.

Eretz Yisrael who serves as a *sheliach tzibbur* in a minyan of b'nei Chutz LaAretz.[29]

Discrepancies in the Torah Reading

14. A ben Eretz Yisrael should not read the Torah on Yom Tov Sheini in Chutz LaAretz[30] but a ben Chutz LaAretz may do so in Eretz Yisrael on the first day of Yom Tov[31] and during Chol HaMoed Sukkos, even though the readings in Eretz Yisrael and Chutz LaAretz differ.[32]

15. When the second day of Shavuos or the eighth day of Pesach falls on Shabbos, a ben Chutz LaAretz may read the Torah for a congregation in Eretz Yisrael, even though the weekly *sidrah* is read whereas in Chutz LaAretz there is a special reading for Yom Tov. He may also read the Torah in subsequent weeks even though different *sidros* are read in Eretz Yisrael and Chutz LaAretz.[33]

16. When the eighth day of Pesach falls on Shabbos, the weekly *sidrah* is read in Eretz Yisrael while the Yom Tov reading is read in

---

29. Ibid.

30. Ibid. Although in certain situations a ben Eretz Yisrael may receive an *aliyah* on Yom Tov Sheini in Chutz LaAretz (see paragraphs 5-7), he may not read the Torah on behalf of b'nei Chutz LaAretz since he is not obligated in that mitzvah.

31. Ibid.

32. See note 26. HaGaon Rav Shlomo Zalman Auerbach explains that since one of the passages read in Chutz LaAretz is also read in Eretz Yisrael, he has the same obligation as the congregation so he may read the Torah for them.

33. This can be inferred from the ruling of HaGaon Rav Moshe Feinstein in note 12. This is also the view of HaGaon Rav Shlomo Zalman Auerbach. It is a mitzvah to read the entire Torah over the year. The fact that for a few weeks different *sidros* are read does not make the basic obligations of a ben Eretz Yisrael and a ben Chutz LaAretz different.

Nevertheless, a ben Eretz Yisrael visiting Chutz LaAretz may not read the Torah on Yom Tov Sheini even when it falls on Shabbos, Monday, or Thursday, when he is obligated in *kerias haTorah*. Moreover, HaGaon Rav Auerbach explains, a ben Eretz Yisrael visiting Chutz LaAretz when Yom Tov Sheini falls on Monday or Thursday has no obligation to listen to the Torah reading of Yom Tov Sheini—the mitzvah to read the Torah is incumbent on the congregation, and since no congregation is reading the weekly *sidrah*, the ben Eretz Yisrael is exempt.

Chutz LaAretz. This results in a discrepancy between the Torah readings in Eretz Yisrael and in Chutz LaAretz for several weeks.[34] B'nei Chutz LaAretz who travel to Eretz Yisrael after Pesach may form a separate minyan on their first Shabbos in the country[35] and read both the sidrah read in Chutz LaAretz that week and the one read in Eretz Yisrael.[36] In many Israeli yeshivos, b'nei Chutz LaAretz read the Yom Tov reading separately and then join the b'nei Eretz Yisrael for the weekly sidrah, thereby circumventing the problem.[37]

A group of people traveling to Eretz Yisrael that week may even form a minyan for minchah on the Shabbos before they leave and read the sidrah they will miss.[38]

---

34. This situation also occurs when Shavuos falls on Friday; that Shabbos, the weekly sidrah is read in Eretz Yisrael, while the Yom Tov reading is read in Chutz LaAretz.

The Torah readings are reconciled by combining either BeHar and BeChukosai, Chukas and Balak, or Matos and Masei in Chutz LaAretz, while splitting them into two sidros in Eretz Yisrael. A local calendar should be consulted in each situation. The details of this procedure are discussed in Maharit, vol. 1, no. 4; Mishnah Berurah 428:10; Ir HaKodesh VeHaMikdash, vol. 3, p. 352; and Sefer Eretz Yisrael, nos. 16, 17, and 20.

35. HaGaon Rav Moshe Feinstein reportedly required b'nei Chutz LaAretz to form their own minyan in Eretz Yisrael when there was a discrepancy in the Torah reading. However, I have heard that HaGaon Rav Elazar Menachem Shach expressed wonder at this report. HaGaon Rav Shlomo Zalman Auerbach also rejected it. Indeed, HaGaon Rav Feinstein's ruling in note 12 contradicts this position. HaRav Dovid Feinstein and HaRav Elimelech Bluth insist that HaGaon Rav Feinstein denied any such obligation. A separate minyan is necessary only when the number of aliyos differs, such as when Yom Tov Sheini falls on a weekday, but not when the reading is different.

36. This is based on a ruling by HaGaon Rav Shlomo Zalman Auerbach. Although HaGaon Rav Yosef Shalom Eliashiv agrees that b'nei Chutz LaAretz have no obligation to form a minyan in order to hear the sidrah they've missed, he considers it preferable for them to do so.

37. BeTzeil HaChochmah, vol. 4, no. 151. When they form a separate minyan for minchah, they should read the Torah as it is read in Chutz LaAretz, although they have already heard the sidrah that morning with the b'nei Eretz Yisrael.

38. HaGaon Rav Moshe Soloveitchik of Zurich reports that this is the custom there. I have also heard that it is customary in Gateshead and London.

17. During these weeks of discrepancy, a ben Eretz Yisrael may be called to the Torah in Chutz LaAretz and vice versa.[39]

Birkas Kohanim

18. Authorities debate whether a ben Eretz Yisrael may recite *birkas kohanim* on Yom Tov Sheini in Chutz LaAretz.[40] Some authorities permit him to do so if no other *kohanim* are present.[41] Others maintain that even in this case he must omit the introductory blessing.[42] A third view advises such a *kohen* to leave the synagogue before the *chazan* begins the blessing of *"Retzei."*[43] Contemporary authorities allow him to recite both *birkas kohanim* and the introductory blessing in all cases.[44]

19. A ben Chutz LaAretz recites *birkas kohanim* every day when he visits Eretz Yisrael.[45]

---

39. This is based on a ruling by HaGaon Rav Shlomo Zalman Auerbach. Also see *Luach Eretz Yisrael* and the Shabbos volume of *Yesodei Yeshurun*, p. 427.

40. *Shaarei Teshuvah* 496:4. A *kohen* who has already recited *birkas kohanim* may repeat it for another congregation (*Rosh HaShanah* 28b), which implies that a *kohen* need not be obligated to recite *birkas kohanim* in order to do so. In the case described in the gemara, however, the *kohen* had been obligated to recite *birkas kohanim* that day but he had already fulfilled his obligation, whereas in our case the *kohen* has no such mitzvah since he does not recite the Yom Tov prayers.

41. *Ginas Veradim* 1:13-14, in the name of Rav Moshe ben Chaviv. Although the Levush questions whether a *kohen* who is repeating *birkas kohanim* may repeat the introductory blessing as well, Rav Moshe ben Chaviv rules that he should.

42. Ibid. Also see *Aruch HaShulchan* 496:5.

43. See *Shulchan Aruch* 128:8 and *Mishnah Berurah* ad loc.; *Teshuvos Chasam Sofer, Orach Chaim*, no. 22.

44. *Be'er Moshe*, pp. 40-47. HaRav Shmuel Feurst writes that this is also the ruling of HaGaon Rav Moshe Feinstein. Also see *Iggeros Moshe* (*Orach Chaim*, vol. 4, no. 106), which states that a ben Eretz Yisrael may help form a minyan on Yom Tov Sheini for both davening and *birkas kohanim*.

45. In Eretz Yisrael, *birkas kohanim* is recited every day. In fact, many authorities discuss why it is not recited daily in Chutz LaAretz. See the Rema, *Orach Chaim* 128:44; *Be'er Moshe*, pp. 42-43; and *Shaarei Yitzchak* 16:9.

CHAPTER 11
"VeSein Tal U'Matar LiVerachah"

Introduction

1. In Eretz Yisrael, the phrase *"vesein tal u'matar liverachah"* (and provide rain and dew for a blessing) is inserted in the *Shemoneh Esrei*—in the blessing of *"Bareich aleinu"*—starting from the seventh of Cheshvan in Eretz Yisrael,[1] and from maariv on December 4th (or December 5th in a leap year) in Chutz LaAretz.[2] In both places, the phrase is said until Pesach.

---

1. *Shulchan Aruch* 117:1. Although the rainy season begins immediately after Sukkos in Eretz Yisrael, we only begin praying for rain two weeks later, in order to allow those who traveled to Yerushalayim for Yom Tov to return home (*Taanis* 10a), and to allow for the completion of the autumn grape harvest.

2. *Shulchan Aruch* 117:1. In Babylonia, the center of the Diaspora in Talmudic times, the rainy season began later than in Eretz Yisrael. See *Mishnah Berurah* ad loc., which explains that the entire Diaspora follows the custom in Babylonia, where people began praying for rain on December 4th.

It should be noted that in his *Commentary on the Mishnah* (*Taanis* 1:3), Rambam rules that each country should pray for rain in accordance with its seasons. In his *Mishneh Torah* (*Hilchos Tefillah* 2:16), however, he agrees that the entire Diaspora follows Babylonia.

Travelers

2. Some authorities rule that if a ben Eretz Yisrael arrives[3] in Chutz LaAretz before the seventh of Cheshvan and intends to return to Eretz Yisrael within a year, or if he travels to Chutz LaAretz for more than a year but has left his family in Eretz Yisrael, he should begin saying *"vesein tal u'matar"* on the seventh of Cheshvan.[4] Others maintain that he should begin on December 4th.[5] Many Sephardic Jews follow the latter view.[6] Alternatively, contemporary authorities advise inserting *"vesein tal u'matar"* in *"Shema koleinu"* rather than *"Bareich aleinu."*[7]

In fact, the Rosh (*Teshuvos HaRosh* 4:10) wonders why each country does not pray for rain as needed. Nevertheless, his objections were not accepted by the other authorities of his generation. See *Hissorerus Teshuvah* (vol. 1, no. 180) and *Shevet HaLevi* (*Orach Chaim*, no. 21), concerning a person who mistakenly inserted *"vesein tal u'matar"* during the summer in a climate that required rain, or one who omitted it during the winter in a country that required no rain.

3. One is considered to have "arrived" as soon as he lands, even before he reaches a Jewish settlement. For the definition of "arriving" with respect to refraining from *melachah* on Yom Tov Sheini, see chapter 4, paragraph 1. Also see *Birkei Yosef* 117:7 and *BeTzeil HaChochmah*, vol. 1, no. 62:3.

4. *Be'er Heiteiv* 117:4. According to *Pri Chadash*, cited in *Pri Megadim*, a ben Eretz Yisrael who plans on remaining in Chutz LaAretz for more than a year should follow the custom of Chutz LaAretz even if he leaves his family in Eretz Yisrael. In *Iggeros Moshe* (*Orach Chaim*, vol. 2, no. 102), HaGaon Rav Moshe Feinstein rules that he should follow the custom of Eretz Yisrael if he travels to a place that needs rain.

5. *Be'er Heiteiv* 117:4, citing Sephardic authorities. *Mishnah Berurah* 117:5 cites this view in the name of *Birkei Yosef*. See *BeTzeil HaChochmah*, vol. 1, no. 62:3.

6. *Ir HaKodesh VeHaMikdash* (vol. 3, chap. 25, no. 1:5) reports that Sephardim follow the Birkei Yosef, who rules that one always upholds the local custom. But see note 7 in the name of HaGaon Rav Ben Tziyon Abba Shaul.

7. HaGaon Rav Shlomo Zalman Auerbach and HaGaon Rav Yosef Shalom Eliashiv explain that this person finds himself in a dilemma: since his home is in Eretz Yisrael, he should begin asking for rain on the seventh of Cheshvan. On the other hand, he should not deviate from the local custom. They resolve this dilemma by advising such a person to recite *"Bareich aleinu"* in accordance with the local custom and insert the request for rain in *"Shema koleinu."* HaGaon Rav Auerbach notes that it makes no difference whether he plans to return to Eretz Yisrael before or after December 4th. *Shaarei Yitzchak* cites *Devar Yehoshua* (vol. 2, no. 14), which reports that this was also the ruling of the Chazon Ish and HaGaon Rav Yoel Teitelbaum of Satmar. HaGaon Rav Ben Tziyon Abba Shaul rules that one should insert the phrase *"vesein tal u'matar be'artzeinu hakedoshah"* in this blessing.

3. A ben Eretz Yisrael who travels to Chutz LaAretz with his family for an extended period begins saying *"vesein tal u'matar"* on December 4th, even if he remains a ben Eretz Yisrael with respect to Yom Tov Sheini.[8] If his family remains in Eretz Yisrael, some authorities rule that he should begin saying it on the seventh of Cheshvan,[9] while others maintain that he starts on December 4th.[10]

4. If a ben Eretz Yisrael travels to Chutz LaAretz after the seventh of Cheshvan and plans to return to Eretz Yisrael after December 4th, he should continue to say *"vesein tal u'matar"* since he began before he left.[11] Some authorities rule that he should insert it in *"Shema koleinu"*—not in *"Bareich aleinu."*[12]

If he does not plan to return, however, he should stop inserting it until December 4th.[13]

One Who Omits *"VeSein Tal U'Matar"*

5. If a ben Eretz Yisrael travels to Chutz LaAretz before December 4th and accidentally omits *"vesein tal u'matar,"* he should insert

---

8. *Iggeros Moshe, Orach Chaim,* vol. 2, no. 102. Since his family has moved with him, he has the same need for rain as b'nei Chutz LaAretz. HaGaon Rav Shlomo Zalman Auerbach, however, questions whether such a person should insert *"vesein tal u'matar"* in *"Shema koleinu"* during the first year of his stay.

9. *Iggeros Moshe, Orach Chaim,* vol. 2, no. 102. Since his family remains in Eretz Yisrael, he needs rain in Eretz Yisrael and should follow the custom of that country.

10. This is based on a ruling by HaGaon Rav Shlomo Zalman Auerbach.

11. *Birkei Yosef* 117:6. This is also the conclusion of *Tzitz Eliezer* (vol. 6, no. 38) and HaGaon Rav Shlomo Zalman Auerbach. If he plans on returning before December 4th, he should certainly not stop inserting *"vesein tal u'matar"* while in Chutz LaAretz. HaGaon Rav Ben Tziyon Abba Shaul reports that this is the Sephardic custom. He adds that a ben Eretz Yisrael should not serve as a *sheliach tzibbur,* even if he is observing a *yahrtzeit,* since he would be forced to deviate from this custom during the repetition of *Shemoneh Esrei.*

12. Based on a ruling by HaGaon Rav Yosef Shalom Eliashiv, this option satisfies all opinions. HaGaon Rav Eliashiv concedes that if he travels for only a week or so, he should continue saying *"vesein tal u'matar"* in *"Bareich aleinu."*

13. *BeTzeil HaChochmah,* vol. 1, no. 62:4; *Shaarei Yitzchak* 13:2.

it in *"Shema koleinu,"* before the words *"ki Atah shomeiah."* If he did not realize his error until after completing that blessing, he need not repeat the *Shemoneh Esrei.*[14]

Serving as a *Sheliach Tzibbur*

6. A ben Eretz Yisrael who travels to Chutz LaAretz between the seventh of Cheshvan and December 4th and is reciting *"vesein tal u'matar"* (see paragraph 4) should not act as a *sheliach tzibbur* during his stay[15] unless he has some reason to do so, e.g., he is observing a *yahrtzeit.*[16] In such a case, he should say *"vesein tal u'matar"* in his silent *Shemoneh Esrei* but omit it in the repetition.[17] Some authorities permit him to serve as a *sheliach tzibbur* even where he has no such reason.[18]

---

14. This is based on a ruling by HaGaon Rav Yosef Shalom Eliashiv. Normally, when a person omits *"vesein tal u'matar"* during the winter, he must repeat the *Shemoneh Esrei,* but since this person may not be obligated to say it during his stay in Chutz LaAretz, he need not repeat the prayer. *BeTzeil HaChochmah* (vol. 1, no. 62:4) arrives at a similar conclusion.

HaGaon Rav Eliashiv adds that although we do not generally recite voluntary prayers, where one might be obligated to repeat the *Shemoneh Esrei,* it is permissible to do so. He should bear in mind that if he is indeed obligated to repeat the *Shemoneh Esrei,* the prayer should fulfill his obligation; otherwise, it should be considered voluntary. See *Mishnah Berurah* 107:2 and *Bei'ur Halachah* ad loc. However, HaGaon Rav Shlomo Zalman Auerbach opposes voluntary prayer even in this situation. See note 23.

15. *BeTzeil HaChochmah,* vol. 1, no. 62:4; *Be'er Moshe,* p. 33, citing *Artzos Ha-Chaim* 10:4. These sources maintain that a *chazan's* silent *Shemoneh Esrei* should not differ from the one he recites for the congregation. Similarly, *Iggeros Moshe* (*Orach Chaim,* vol. 2, no. 29) rules that if a *chazan* prays according to *nusach Ashkenaz* and is asked to serve as the *chazan* in a synagogue that follows *nusach Sephard,* he should recite the silent *Shemoneh Esrei* in accordance with *nusach Sephard.*

16. *Be'er Moshe,* p. 26. See note 7 for the Sephardic practice.

17. *Birkei Yosef* 117:8.

18. This is based on a ruling by HaGaon Rav Shlomo Zalman Auerbach and HaGaon Rav Yosef Shalom Eliashiv.

Visiting Eretz Yisrael

7. Some authorities rule that if a ben Chutz LaAretz arrives in Eretz Yisrael before the seventh of Cheshvan and plans to return to Chutz LaAretz within the year, or if he intends to stay in Eretz Yisrael for more than a year but has left his family in Chutz LaAretz, he is subject to the two views cited in paragraph 2.[19] Others maintain that according to everyone, he begins saying *"vesein tal u'matar"* on the seventh of Cheshvan—even if he will return to Chutz LaAretz before December 4th.[20]

Contemporary authorities conclude that if he is leaving Eretz Yisrael after December 4th, he should begin saying *"vesein tal u'matar"* on the seventh of Cheshvan; otherwise, he should insert it in *"Shema koleinu."*[21]

If he accidentally omitted *"vesein tal u'matar,"* if he intends to leave Eretz Yisrael after December 4th he must repeat the *Shemoneh Esrei;*[22] otherwise, he need not repeat it.[23]

8. If a ben Chutz LaAretz visits Eretz Yisrael and begins to say *"vesein tal u'matar"*—either in *"Bareich aleinu"* or in *"Shema koleinu"*—

---

19. This is implied by the words of the Mishnah Berurah (117:5), based on the Pri Megadim.

20. *BeTzeil HaChochmah*, vol. 1, no. 62:4, citing *Pri Chadash*. The author compares such a person to someone from a place where people don't fast on a particular day: if he comes to a place where people do fast, he must fast with them. Similarly, a visitor from Chutz LaAretz should participate in the local prayers for rain. Also see *Shaarei Yitzchak* 13:3.

21. HaGaon Rav Shlomo Zalman Auerbach explains that the Mishnah Berurah uses the term "year" loosely, referring not to a conventional year but to the period ending December 4th. The obligation to recite *"vesein tal u'matar"* depends not on one's permanent place of residence but on where one will be between the seventh of Cheshvan and December 4th. If he plans to return before December 4th, his status is in doubt and he should insert *"vesein tal u'matar"* in *"Shema koleinu."* HaGaon Rav Yosef Shalom Eliashiv and HaGaon Rav Ben Tziyon Abba Shaul concur.

22. *BeTzeil HaChochmah*, vol. 1, no. 62. If one intends to remain in Eretz Yisrael until December 4th, it is considered as if he is residing there the entire year. See note 21.

23. HaGaon Rav Shlomo Zalman Auerbach rules that he should not even recite a voluntary *Shemoneh Esrei*, whereas HaGaon Rav Yosef Shalom Eliashiv permits him to do so. See note 14.

he should stop reciting it if he returns to Chutz LaAretz before December 4th.[24]

9. A ben Chutz LaAretz who travels to Eretz Yisrael between the seventh of Cheshvan and December 4th and is not saying *"vesein tal u'matar"* should not serve as a *sheliach tzibbur* during his visit unless he has some reason to do so, e.g., he is observing a *yahrtzeit*.[25] In such a case, he should omit *"vesein tal u'matar"* in his *Shemoneh Esrei* but recite it during the repetition. Others maintain that he may be a *sheliach tzibbur* even when he has no such reason.[26]

10. A ben Chutz LaAretz who has decided to move to Eretz Yisrael, or a ben Eretz Yisrael who has decided to move to Chutz LaAretz, does not change his practice regarding the recitation of *"vesein tal u'matar"* until he actually moves.[27]

"Morid HaTal"

11. If a ben Chutz LaAretz settles in Eretz Yisrael during the summer, he should begin to insert the words *"Morid hatal"* in the blessing of *"Mechayeih hameisim."*[28] If he visits Eretz Yisrael during the summer, he may do so if he wishes. If he serves as a *sheliach tzibbur*, he should insert it during the repetition of the *Shemoneh Esrei.*[29]

12. If a ben Eretz Yisrael moves to a community in Chutz LaAretz where people do not recite *"Morid hatal,"* he may stop saying it. If he visits such a place, he should continue saying it. If he serves as a *sheliach tzibbur*, he should say it in his silent *Shemoneh Esrei* but omit it during the repetition.[30]

---

24. *BeTzeil HaChochmah*, vol. 1, no. 62.; *Be'er Moshe*, p. 27.

25. *Shaarei Yitzchak* 13:4. See *Iggeros Moshe, Orach Chaim*, vol. 2, no. 29.

26. This is based on a ruling by HaGaon Rav Yosef Shalom Eliashiv.

27. This is based on a ruling by HaGaon Rav Shlomo Zalman Auerbach.

28. This is based on a ruling by HaGaon Rav Shlomo Zalman Auerbach. Since residents of Eretz Yisrael recite *"Morid hatal,"* a person who settles there must adopt the local custom.

29. This is based on a ruling by HaGaon Rav Shlomo Zalman Auerbach.

30. Ibid.

CHAPTER 12
Bris Milah and Sheva Berachos

A *Bris Milah* Performed on Time

1. Some authorities permit a ben Chutz LaAretz to perform a *bris milah* that is taking place on time (i.e., eight days after birth) on Yom Tov Sheini in Eretz Yisrael, even if a *mohel* who is a ben Eretz Yisrael is available. Others rule that the ben Eretz Yisrael should be employed.[1]

2. When a *bris milah* is performed on time on Yom Tov Sheini in Chutz LaAretz, there is no advantage to using a *mohel* who is visiting from Eretz Yisrael.[2]

---

1. *Shaarei Teshuvah* (496:5) and *Birkei Yosef* (*Orach Chaim* 331:4) cite a dispute among the early authorities regarding this issue. The Birkei Yosef himself rules stringently. Although *milah* is performed even on Shabbos, it still might be preferable to use a *mohel* who is not observing Yom Tov. But *Be'er Moshe* (pp. 240-242) and HaGaon Rav Shlomo Zalman Auerbach rule leniently.

2. This is based on a ruling by HaGaon Rav Shlomo Zalman Auerbach. Being particular to use a ben Eretz Yisrael would constitute a degradation of Yom Tov.

A Postponed *Bris Milah*

3. A *bris milah* that has been postponed may not be performed on Yom Tov Sheini in Chutz LaAretz.[3] In Eretz Yisrael, a local *mohel* may perform the *bris*. If none is available, some authorities permit a ben Chutz LaAretz to serve as the *mohel*,[4] while others do not.[5]

4. If a ben Chutz LaAretz is visiting Eretz Yisrael, he should appoint a local *mohel* to perform his son's *bris* on Yom Tov Sheini.[6]

5. A postponed *bris milah* may not be performed in Chutz LaAretz on Yom Tov Sheini, even by a ben Eretz Yisrael.[7]

Sheva Berachos

6. As explained in chapter 6, paragraph 10, when a ben Chutz LaAretz marries a bas Eretz Yisrael in Eretz Yisrael and they plan to move to Chutz LaAretz soon after the wedding, the groom remains a ben Chutz LaAretz. Therefore, if one of the days of their *sheva berachos* occurs on Yom Tov Sheini, they do not have to invite

---

3. See chapter 1, paragraph 18.

4. This is based on a ruling by HaGaon Rav Shlomo Zalman Auerbach. Since some authorities permit a postponed *bris milah* to be performed on Yom Tov Sheini, and some rule that once the *bris* can be performed from a medical point of view, every day of needless postponement abrogates a positive commandment, we may rely on the Chacham Tzvi (no. 167), who allows all residents of Chutz LaAretz to observe one day of Yom Tov in Eretz Yisrael. Also see *Shaarei Yitzchak* 16.

5. This is based on a ruling by HaGaon Rav Yosef Shalom Eliashiv, who disregards the Chacham Tzvi.

6. *Sdeh Chemed, Maareches Yom Tov* 1:10, citing *VaYaan Avraham*, no. 21. This is also the ruling of HaGaon Rav Shlomo Zalman Auerbach. Although HaGaon Rav Yosef Shalom Eliashiv forbids a ben Chutz LaAretz to perform a *bris* on Yom Tov Sheini, he considers it a mitzvah for the father to appoint a ben Eretz Yisrael to serve as the *mohel*.

7. *Be'er Moshe*, p. 242; *Shaarei Yitzchak* 16:3. Using a ben Eretz Yisrael to perform the *bris* would involve a degradation of Yom Tov. See note 2 and chapter 1, paragraph 18.

someone who was not at the wedding in order to recite the *sheva berachos*, even if all the guests except the groom are b'nei Eretz Yisrael.[8]

7. As also explained in chapter 6, if a ben Chutz LaAretz marries a bas Eretz Yisrael in Chutz LaAretz and they plan to move to Eretz Yisrael, the groom remains a ben Chutz LaAretz until they move. Thus, in this case as well there is no need for *panim chadashos* on Yom Tov Sheini.[9]

8. The above ruling also applies to a ben Eretz Yisrael who marries a bas Chutz LaAretz in Chutz LaAretz and plans to move to Eretz Yisrael after the wedding: since the bride remains a bas Chutz LaAretz until they move, there is no need for *panim chadashos* on Yom Tov Sheini.[10]

But if a ben Eretz Yisrael marries a bas Chutz LaAretz in Eretz Yisrael and they plan to move to Chutz LaAretz after the wedding, if seven men at the meal are b'nei Chutz LaAretz, there is no need for *panim chadashos*; if there are fewer than seven b'nei Chutz LaAretz, however, a halachic authority should be consulted.[11]

---

8. During the week of *sheva berachos*, seven special blessings are recited whenever the bride and groom eat together with at least ten men, provided that one of them is a "new face" (*panim chadashos*) who was not at the wedding. On Shabbos, however, the sanctity of the day provides the *panim chadashos* and the blessings are recited in any case. Likewise on Yom Tov, even if the groom is observing the day but the bride is not. See *BeTzeil HaChochmah* (vol. 1, no. 64), which cites the Ran's view that the *sheva berachos* reflect the joy in the groom's heart. Also see the *Shulchan Aruch* (*Even HaEzer* 62:2), which states that Yom Tov Sheini, too, is considered *panim chadashos*.

9. *BeTzeil HaChochmah*, vol. 1, no. 64, par. 5.

10. Ibid., par. 3, based on the Ritva (*Kesubos* 7a), who explains that the blessings are based on the joy of both the bride and the groom, and it is also Yom Tov for the participants.

11. Ibid., par. 4, since it is not Yom Tov for all the participants, and the Ran maintains that the blessings only reflect the joy of the groom.

CHAPTER 13
Eulogies, Mourning, and *Yizkor*

Eulogies

1. A ben Chutz LaAretz may not attend a eulogy for a Torah scholar in Eretz Yisrael on Yom Tov Sheini.[1] But he may attend the funeral and serve as a pallbearer.[2]

---

1. *Iggeros Moshe, Orach Chaim,* vol. 3, no. 77. Although Chazal permitted funerals on Yom Tov Sheini (*Beitzah* 6a), eulogies are forbidden. Therefore, a person who is observing Yom Tov may not participate in the eulogy.

Eulogies are normally forbidden on Chol HaMoed and *issru chag* (the day following Yom Tov), but it is occasionally permitted to eulogize an outstanding Torah scholar on *issru chag*. See *Mishnah Berurah* 547:12, in the name of *Magen Avraham*; *Panim Meiros*, vol. 2, no. 48; *Teshuvos Chasam Sofer, Orach Chaim,* no. 103; and *Toras Rephael*, no. 78. Although the *Shulchan Aruch* (*Yoreh Deah* 401:1) permits the eulogizing of a great Torah scholar even on Chol HaMoed, *Mishnah Berurah* (547:12) points out that today no Torah scholar is great enough to merit such special consideration. *Teshuvah MeAhavah* (vol. 1, no. 207) allows for the eulogizing of any leading Torah figure.

In certain situations, the deceased may be praised on Chol HaMoed in such a way that the congregation will not be reduced to tears. HaGaon Rav Shlomo Zalman Auerbach has written me that a ben Chutz LaAretz may listen to such praise on Yom Tov Sheini.

2. *Iggeros Moshe, Orach Chaim,* vol. 3, no. 77.

Yizkor

2. A ben Chutz LaAretz davening in Eretz Yisrael with a minyan of b'nei Eretz Yisrael should not recite Yizkor with them on the first day of Yom Tov. Rather, he should recite it in a minyan of b'nei Chutz LaAretz on Yom Tov Sheini.[3] If he cannot attend such a minyan, some authorities rule that he should recite Yizkor on the first day of Yom Tov.[4]

3. In Chutz LaAretz, a ben Eretz Yisrael should recite Yizkor privately on the seventh day of Pesach and the first day of Shavuos.[5] If he attends services on Yom Tov Sheini and says Yizkor then, however, he is to be praised.[6] If so, he should arrive for the beginning of services, as if he is participating in the Yom Tov prayers.[7]

---

3. BeTzeil HaChochmah, vol. 4, no. 120. The author limits this ruling to one who is accustomed to reciting Yizkor in Chutz LaAretz. But one who is reciting Yizkor for the first time may do so on the first day of Yom Tov. HaGaon Rav Shlomo Zalman Auerbach points out that although it is preferable to recite Yizkor with a minyan, one may do so privately as well. Gesher HaChaim (chap. 31, par. 2) cites a similar ruling in the name of Dudaei HaSadeh.

4. Rivevos Ephraim (342:2) explains that Yizkor may be recited on either day of Yom Tov. HaRav Shmuel Feurst has written me that he also heard this ruling from HaGaon Rav Moshe Feinstein. But according to BeTzeil HaChochmah, as cited in note 3, a person who has begun to recite Yizkor on Yom Tov Sheini must continue this practice, even if he will have to recite it privately.

   Although congregants not saying Yizkor generally leave the synagogue when it is recited, HaGaon Rav Shlomo Zalman Auerbach has written to me that when a ben Chutz LaAretz visits Eretz Yisrael and will say Yizkor on Yom Tov Sheini, he need not leave the synagogue when it is recited on the first day of Yom Tov.

5. This question does not arise on the last day of Sukkos since Yizkor is recited on Shemini Atzeres (the first of the last two days of Yom Tov) even in Chutz LaAretz. See Iggeros Moshe, vol. 3, no. 95; Kol Bo Al Aveilus, p. 403; and BeTzeil HaChochmah, vol. 4, no. 119.

6. BeTzeil HaChochmah, vol. 4, no. 119. If one will be missed if he does not attend services on Yom Tov Sheini, he must do so in any case. See chapter 4, paragraph 6.

7. See chapter 4, paragraph 6.

CHAPTER 14
Performing *Melachah* for a Ben Chutz LaAretz

A Ben Eretz Yisrael in Chutz LaAretz

1. A ben Chutz LaAretz may not ask a visitor from Eretz Yisrael to perform *melachah* for him on Yom Tov Sheini, nor may the visitor volunteer to do so.[1]

A Ben Chutz LaAretz in Eretz Yisrael

2. According to most authorities, a ben Chutz LaAretz may not ask a ben Eretz Yisrael to perform *melachah* for him on Yom Tov

---

[1]. *Teshuvos HaRadvaz* (no. 1329) compares this to the prohibition of asking a non-Jew to perform *melachah* on Yom Tov. Moreover, it will certainly lead to a degradation of Yom Tov. Radvaz adds that the host must even object if a ben Eretz Yisrael undertakes to perform *melachah* on his behalf. Also see *Iggeros Moshe, Orach Chaim*, vol. 2, no. 106.

Sheini[2]—even by way of a direct hint,[3] and even if he asks before Yom Tov.[4] If he asked nonetheless, the ben Eretz Yisrael may not oblige him. But if a ben Eretz Yisrael performs *melachah*, a ben Chutz LaAretz may derive benefit from it.[5]

3. A ben Chutz LaAretz may ask a ben Eretz Yisrael to perform any *melachah* permissible on Yom Tov, such as cooking.[6] But if this will lead the ben Eretz Yisrael to do something prohibited on Yom Tov, such as striking a match to light the stove, some authorities forbid the request,[7] while others allow it.[8]

---

2. *Shaarei Teshuvah* 496, citing *Mahari Farrago, Mahari Molko,* and *Ginas Veradim*. This is also the conclusion of R. Akiva Eiger and *Chochmas Shlomo,* in their glosses on the *Shulchan Aruch* 49, and of *Pe'as HaShulchan* 2:15. Contemporary authorities concur. See *Doveiv Meisharim,* vol. 3, no. 83; *Iggeros Moshe, Orach Chaim,* vol. 3, no. 73, and vol. 4, nos. 105-107; and *Minchas Yitzchak,* vol. 7, nos. 34-35. This is the ruling of HaGaon Rav Shlomo Zalman Auerbach and HaGaon Rav Yosef Shalom Eliashiv as well.

3. This is based on a ruling by HaGaon Rav Shlomo Zalman Auerbach. Hinting is forbidden only when a request is implied, such as pointing to a light switch. But hinting without specifically requesting anything, such as saying, "It's dark in my room," is permitted. Similarly, if a host asks his guest from Chutz LaAretz if he would like him to turn on the light, the guest may respond in the affirmative, since he did not initiate the request. Similar rules apply to asking a non-Jew to do *melachah* on Shabbos and Yom Tov. See *Shulchan Aruch* 307:22 and *Mishnah Berurah* ad loc.

4. *Iggeros Moshe, Orach Chaim,* vol. 4, no. 195:1. However, see the view of Ha-Gaon Rav Yosef Shalom Eliashiv cited in note 8.

5. This is based on rulings by HaGaon Rav Shlomo Zalman Auerbach and HaGaon Rav Yosef Shalom Eliashiv, who allow a ben Chutz LaAretz to request that a ben Eretz Yisrael perform *melachah* for him in a time of great need. But see *Minchas Yitzchak,* vol. 7, nos. 34-35, and *Chochmas Shlomo* on *Shulchan Aruch* 469.

6. Just as he may perform the act himself, he may ask a ben Eretz Yisrael to do it for him.

7. This is the view of HaGaon Rav Yosef Shalom Eliashiv. Since the host must perform an action forbidden on Yom Tov in order to fulfill his guest's request, it is as if the guest asked him to perform the *melachah*.

8. This is the view of HaGaon Rav Shlomo Zalman Auerbach, since the guest does not explicitly ask his host to perform an action forbidden on Yom Tov.

4. A ben Eretz Yisrael may perform *melachah* on his own initiative for a ben Chutz LaAretz in Eretz Yisrael.[9]

Traveling

5. A ben Chutz LaAretz visiting Eretz Yisrael may not travel in a car driven by a ben Eretz Yisrael on Yom Tov Sheini. Nor may he may board a bus even if a ben Eretz Yisrael pays his fare.[10]

Employment

6. A ben Chutz LaAretz who owns a business in Eretz Yisrael may employ b'nei Eretz Yisrael on Yom Tov Sheini, provided that they are hired on a weekly or monthly basis rather than a daily one.[11] Some authorities permit this arrangement only if the business is co-owned by a ben Eretz Yisrael or a non-Jew.[12]

In his responsa printed in the Hebrew edition of this book (pp. 218-229), HaGaon Rav Yosef Shalom Eliashiv permits a ben Chutz LaAretz to ask a ben Eretz Yisrael to perform *melachah* when it is needed for the performance of a mitzvah. HaGaon Rav Auerbach, however, disagrees (see p. 151, note 10).

9. *Minchas Yitzchak*, vol. 7, nos. 34-35. This is also the view of HaGaon Rav Shlomo Zalman Auerbach and HaGaon Rav Yosef Shalom Eliashiv. The prohibition applies only when the ben Eretz Yisrael serves as an agent of the ben Chutz LaAretz—not when he acts on his own initiative.

10. HaGaon Rav Shlomo Zalman Auerbach and HaGaon Rav Yosef Shalom Eliashiv consider this a serious degradation of Yom Tov.

11. *Iggeros Moshe, Orach Chaim*, vol. 2, no. 99, and vol. 3, no. 71; *Chelkas Yaacov*, vol. 3, nos. 27-28; *Shemiras Shabbos KeHilchasah*, chap. 31, note 80, citing HaGaon Rav Shlomo Zalman Auerbach; and *Minchas Shlomo*, no. 19:3. *Minchas Shlomo* further permits a Jew living in Eretz Yisrael to do *melachah* after Shabbos on behalf of a Jew living in Chutz LaAretz, even though it is still Shabbos there.

12. *Birkei Yosef, Orach Chaim* 496:5; *Pe'as HaShulchan* 2:15; *Doveiv Meisharim*, vol. 3, no. 83; *Kaf HaChaim, Orach Chaim* 496:45. Also see *Minchas Yitzchak*, vol. 7, no. 34; *Be'er Moshe*, p. 153; *BeTzeil HaChochmah*, vol. 3, no. 125.

7. It is questionable whether a ben Eretz Yisrael who owns a factory in Chutz LaAretz may have non-Jews work for him on Yom Tov Sheini. A halachic authority should be consulted.[13]

---

13. In *Minchas Shlomo* (no. 19:3), HaGaon Rav Shlomo Zalman Auerbach rules that if the factory is not known to be owned by a Jew, it is certainly permitted. A halachic authority must therefore determine whether the factory in question is indeed "known."

CHAPTER 15
Performing *Melachah* for a Ben Eretz Yisrael

Introduction

It is forbidden to cook or expend any extra effort (even if it does not involve *melachah*) on Yom Tov for the needs of the week. Since Yom Tov Sheini is a weekday for a ben Eretz Yisrael, authorities discuss whether a ben Chutz LaAretz may cook on that day for b'nei Eretz Yisrael. Their conclusions are presented below.

A Ben Eretz Yisrael Visiting Chutz LaAretz

1. Although a ben Eretz Yisrael visiting Chutz LaAretz may not perform *melachah* on Yom Tov Sheini (even privately), when Yom Tov Sheini falls on Friday, he may cook for Shabbos without setting aside an *eiruv tavshilin* before Yom Tov.[1]

---

1. See chapter 4, note 5. A visitor from Eretz Yisrael may not perform *melachah* on Yom Tov Sheini lest he arouse dissent (*Mishnah Berurah* 468:17). Since b'nei Chutz LaAretz may cook for Shabbos, albeit with an *eiruv tavshilin*, when a ben Eretz Yisrael cooks without one it will not arouse dissent, for any observer will assume that either he did set one aside or he is relying on someone else's. See *Teshuvos HaRadvaz*, vol. 4, no. 73, quoted in *Magen Avraham* 496:7; and *Mishnah Berurah* 496:13.

2. A ben Chutz LaAretz may cook for a ben Eretz Yisrael on Yom Tov Sheini if he cooks his guest's food together with his own in the same pot.[2] He may even prepare a separate dish in honor of his guest, provided that he or another ben Chutz LaAretz eats it as well.[3] Some authorities allow cooking for a ben Eretz Yisrael without these stipulations.[4]

A Ben Chutz LaAretz in Eretz Yisrael

3. A ben Chutz LaAretz visiting Eretz Yisrael may perform any *melachah* permitted on Yom Tov Sheini; he need not ask a ben Eretz Yisrael to perform these *melachos* for him.[5]

4. Some authorities rule that a ben Chutz LaAretz visiting Eretz Yisrael should not cook for a ben Eretz Yisrael in a separate pot,[6]

---

2. *Mahari Tatz* (vol. 1, no. 139) examines whether the license given by the Torah to cook on Yom Tov includes cooking for someone who is not required to observe Yom Tov that day. In any case, one may add food to his pot for the needs of such a person; it is even permissible to add food for after Yom Tov if the addition will enhance the Yom Tov food.

3. Ibid.

4. *Mahari Tatz* offers several reasons why cooking for a ben Eretz Yisrael may be permitted in any case: since a host must provide food for his guests, cooking for them may be considered a Yom Tov need; in addition, it is a mitzvah to celebrate Chol HaMoed and *issru chag* with a festive meal; and since a ben Eretz Yisrael may not perform *melachah* in Chutz LaAretz on Yom Tov Sheini, it is, in a sense, Yom Tov for him as well. This responsum is cited in *Pischei Teshuvah* on *Shulchan Aruch* 496 and *Kaf HaChaim, Orach Chaim* 496:7, and most authorities rule leniently in this matter. See *She'eilas Yaavetz*, no. 168; R. Akiva Eiger, *Derush VeChiddush, Kesubos, Maarachah* 16; HaGaon Rav Tzvi Pesach Frank, *Mikraei Kodesh*, Pesach, vol. 2, no. 59; and *Bei'ur Halachah* 512:1, s.v. "*Ein.*" This is also the conclusion of HaGaon Rav Yosef Shalom Eliashiv and HaGaon Rav Shlomo Zalman Auerbach. HaGaon Rav Auerbach, however, prefers one of the two solutions offered in the text where this does not present hardship.

5. *Be'er Moshe*, pp. 241-242.

6. See note 4 for three reasons why a ben Chutz LaAretz may cook for a ben Eretz Yisrael on Yom Tov Sheini in Chutz LaAretz. In *Mikraei Kodesh* (Pesach, vol. 2, no. 59), HaGaon Rav Tzvi Pesach Frank notes that only the second reason applies in Eretz Yisrael. He concludes, therefore, that Mahari Tatz would not permit a ben Chutz LaAretz to cook for a ben Eretz Yisrael on Yom Tov Sheini in Eretz Yisrael. This is also the ruling of HaGaon Rav Shlomo Zalman Auerbach.

while others permit him to do so.[7] Even those who rule stringently allow a ben Chutz LaAretz to cook for a sick or elderly person who cannot cook for himself,[8] but it is preferable for the ben Chutz LaAretz to taste the food.[9]

Cooking on Chol HaMoed

5.   In Chutz LaAretz, a ben Eretz Yisrael may not cook for Yom Tov Sheini on Chol HaMoed, whether for himself[10] or for b'nei Chutz LaAretz.[11] But in Eretz Yisrael, he may do so for b'nei Chutz LaAretz.[12]

---

7. *Mikraei Kodesh*, Pesach, vol. 2, no. 59, based on R. Akiva Eiger as cited in note 4. This is also the view of HaGaon Rav Yosef Shalom Eliashiv.

8. HaGaon Rav Shlomo Zalman Auerbach explains that if the elderly person has no one else to prepare food for him, the ben Chutz LaAretz must not let him go hungry. Cooking for him is therefore a Yom Tov need.

9. HaGaon Rav Shlomo Zalman Auerbach notes that this way, the food will not be exclusively for the ben Eretz Yisrael.

10. See R. Akiva Eiger's glosses on *Shulchan Aruch* 496, also cited by *Kaf HaChaim*, *Orach Chaim* 539:62. When a ben Eretz Yisrael cooks on Chol HaMoed for Yom Tov Sheini, he is actually cooking for a weekday since he only refrains from *melachah* on that day in order to avoid controversy.

11. This is based on a ruling by HaGaon Rav Shlomo Zalman Auerbach.

12. *Harirei Kodesh* on *Mikraei Kodesh*, Pesach, vol. 2, p. 198. Whatever a ben Chutz LaAretz may do for himself on Chol HaMoed, e.g., cooking for Yom Tov Sheini, others may do for him as well. Although HaGaon Rav Shlomo Zalman Auerbach questions this reasoning, he permits cooking for a ben Chutz LaAretz on Chol HaMoed for Yom Tov Sheini because a host is obligated to enable his guests from Chutz LaAretz to rejoice on both days of Yom Tov; cooking for them is therefore a bona fide Yom Tov need. Nevertheless, HaGaon Rav Auerbach limits this permission to a case where the ben Chutz LaAretz is a guest of a ben Eretz Yisrael and it would be difficult for him to cook for himself. But according to *Harirei Kodesh*, cooking would be permitted in any case.

CHAPTER 16
Muktzeh

A Ben Eretz Yisrael in Chutz LaAretz

1. A ben Eretz Yisrael visiting Chutz LaAretz on Yom Tov Sheini may not move objects that are obviously *muktzeh*, such as coins, paper money, or broken utensils,[1] even if he moves them discreetly.[2]

2. A *kli shemelachto le'issur*—any utensil usually used to perform an act forbidden on Yom Tov (e.g., a hammer)[3]—may be moved on Yom Tov if it is being used to perform a permissible act (e.g., cracking a nut), or if one needs the space. Such utensils may be moved on Yom Tov Sheini by a ben Eretz Yisrael even where no such need exists,[4] provided that they belong to a ben Eretz Yisrael.

---

1. *BeTzeil HaChochmah*, vol. 1, no. 39.

2. HaGaon Rav Shlomo Zalman Auerbach has written me that if something is not known to be *muktzeh*, a ben Eretz Yisrael may handle it on Yom Tov Sheini. For example, he may handle fruit that fell from a tree on Yom Tov since any observer will assume that it fell beforehand and is therefore not *muktzeh*. This is also the view of HaGaon Rav Yosef Shalom Eliashiv and HaGaon Rav Shmuel HaLevi Wosner. Also see *BeTzeil HaChochmah*, vol. 1, no. 39:7.

3. See *Shulchan Aruch* 308:3.

4. See note 2.

3. Some authorities allow a ben Eretz Yisrael to handle sukkah decorations on Simchas Torah.[5] Others disagree.[6]

A Ben Chutz LaAretz in Eretz Yisrael

4. A ben Chutz LaAretz visiting Eretz Yisrael may not move any *muktzeh* object on Yom Tov Sheini.[7] According to most authorities, this includes tefillin.[8]

---

5. This is based on a ruling by HaGaon Rav Shlomo Zalman Auerbach.

6. This is based on a ruling by HaGaon Rav Yosef Shalom Eliashiv. Since the decorations remain *muktzeh* for their owner, they are *muktzeh* for his guest as well.

7. *BeTzeil HaChochmah*, vol. 1, no. 39:7.

8. See chapter 8, paragraph 4. Since most authorities do not allow a ben Chutz LaAretz to wear tefillin on Yom Tov Sheini in Eretz Yisrael, *Chelkas Yaacov* (vol. 3, no. 154) concludes that he should not handle them either. But in those instances in which HaGaon Rav Shlomo Zalman Auerbach permits b'nei Chutz LaAretz to wear tefillin (see chapter 8, note 8), obviously they are allowed to handle them.

CHAPTER 17
Selling *Chametz*

1. A ben Eretz Yisrael spending Pesach in a country west of Eretz Yisrael, such as the United States,[1] must sell his *chametz* before Pesach begins in Eretz Yisrael, and may not reacquire it until Pesach ends in Chutz LaAretz.[2]

---

1. This question also arises when a person in the eastern part of the United States spends Pesach in the west, since Pesach begins three hours earlier in New York than in Los Angeles.

Beginning at midday on *erev Pesach*, the Torah forbids one to eat or derive benefit from *chametz*. Rabbinic law extends these prohibitions to two hours before midday and one hour before midday, respectively. See *Pesachim* 11b, 28b; and Rambam, *Mishneh Torah, Hilchos Chametz U'Matzah* 1:7. In addition, the Sages declared that any *chametz* owned by a Jew during Pesach is forbidden forever. See *Pesachim* 29a-30a.

Contemporary authorities debate whether these prohibitions depend on what time it is in the place where the *chametz* is located, or what time it is in the place where the owner of the *chametz* finds himself. Based on *Pesachim* 31a, *Oneg Yom Tov* (no. 36) deems the location of the *chametz* the determining factor, but later authorities conclude the opposite. See *Mikraei Kodesh*, Pesach, no. 55; *Minchas Yitzchak*, vol. 7, no. 25; *Mishnas Yaavetz, Orach Chaim*, no. 13:1; and *Moadim U'Zemanim*, vol. 3, no. 269. Nevertheless, *Minchas Yitzchak* and *Iggeros Moshe* (*Orach Chaim*, vol. 4, nos. 94-95) recommend that both views be taken into account.

2. *Iggeros Moshe, Orach Chaim*, vol. 4, nos. 94-95. Even if the rav acting as his agent repurchases the chametz immediately after Pesach in Eretz Yisrael, the owner does not acquire title until Pesach ends in Chutz LaAretz.

2. A person who lives west of Eretz Yisrael[3] and spends Pesach in Eretz Yisrael should sell his *chametz* in Eretz Yisrael,[4] reacquiring it following the eighth day of Pesach.[5]

3. If a ben Chutz LaAretz goes to Eretz Yisrael for Pesach and leaves his family at home, he should give his *chametz* to a family member,[6] instructing him to either sell it or give it away.[7]

4. Once *chametz* becomes forbidden in Eretz Yisrael, if a ben Chutz LaAretz visiting there remembers that he owns *chametz* in Chutz LaAretz, that *chametz* may never be used, even if he remem-

---

It should be noted that HaGaon Rav Betzalel Zolty rejects the view of *Oneg Yom Tov* completely and permits a person leaving Eretz Yisrael to sell his *chametz* on *erev Pesach* in Chutz LaAretz (*Mishnas Yaavetz, Orach Chaim,* no. 13:1).

3. Likewise, a person who lives in the western part of the United States and spends Pesach in the east should sell his *chametz* in the place where Pesach begins earlier. See *Moadim U'Zemanim,* vol. 3, no. 269.

4. See notes 1-2 in the name of *Iggeros Moshe.* Also see *Mikraei Kodesh,* vol. 1, p. 162.

5. *Iggeros Moshe, Orach Chaim,* vol. 4, nos. 94-95.
In fact, the sales contract found in *Mikraei Kodesh* (Pesach, no. 66) states that all *chametz* is repurchased by the Jew immediately after Pesach ends in Eretz Yisrael, "with the exception of *chametz* owned by b'nei Chutz LaAretz." The *beis din* of HaGaon Rav Nissim Karelitz of B'nei Brak draws up separate contracts for b'nei Eretz Yisrael and b'nei Chutz LaAretz. HaGaon Rav Moshe Halbershtam has told me that in Yerushalayim it is customary to sell *chametz* for ten days—in order to include *chametz* in the Far East, as was the custom of HaGaon Rav Pinchas Epstein in the previous generation.
According to *Siddur Pesach KeHilchaso* (chap. 11), even if such a tourist appoints a rav to sell his *chametz* but neglects to instruct him to repurchase it only after the eighth day of Pesach, the ben Chutz LaAretz is considered not to have reacquired the *chametz* until that time, for we assume that this was his intention. *Iggeros Moshe* offers an alternative resolution: since Yom Tov Sheini is a rabbinic enactment and so is the prohibition against using *chametz* owned by a Jew during Pesach, we can rely on the fact that Pesach actually ends after the seventh day even for b'nei Chutz LaAretz. This is also the view of HaGaon Rav Tzvi Pesach Frank (*Mikraei Kodesh,* Pesach, no. 76). But see *Hissorerus Teshuvah,* vol. 2, no. 179.

6. *Minchas Yitzchak,* vol. 7, no. 25.

7. Ibid.

bered before *chametz* became forbidden in Chutz LaAretz.[8] Yet some authorities maintain that even if Pesach has begun in Eretz Yisrael, as long as he reminded himself before the sixth hour of the day in the place where the *chametz* is located, he may recite the *bitul* (nullification) declaration, renouncing ownership of the *chametz* and rendering it permissible after Pesach.[9]

5. If a ben Eretz Yisrael visiting Chutz LaAretz realizes before the sixth hour that he has forgotten to sell his *chametz* in Eretz Yisrael, he may still renounce ownership by reciting the *bitul* declaration.[10]

---

8. As stated in note 1, most authorities agree that the determining factor is where the owner of the *chametz* is located—not where the *chametz* is. See *Iggeros Moshe, Orach Chaim*, vol. 4, nos. 94-95.

9. This is the ruling of HaGaon Rav Y. M. Tokichinsky (*HaYomam* 26:9) according to the opinion that the determining factor is the location of the *chametz*. In cases of substantial loss, one should consult a rabbinical authority as to the status of such *chametz*.

10. Ibid. See *Mikraei Kodesh*, Pesach, no. 76.

CHAPTER 18
The Boundaries
of Eretz Yisrael

Introduction

When the Sanhedrin sat in Yerushalayim, Rosh Chodesh was determined by the sighting of the new moon by two witnesses. Once these witnesses were accepted by the Sanhedrin, messengers were dispatched to announce which day had been declared Rosh Chodesh. In those locales too distant to be reached by messenger before Yom Tov, the Jews observed two days of Yom Tov out of doubt. Even after the Sanhedrin was exiled and Jews began to observe Rosh Chodesh based on the calculations that form the backbone of the present-day Jewish calendar, Jews in distant places continued to observe two days of Yom Tov, in accordance with the enactment of Chazal (*Beitzah* 4b).

Authorities dispute the exact boundaries included in the enactment of Yom Tov Sheini. Some maintain that one day of Yom Tov is observed throughout Eretz Yisrael (i.e., the land conquered by the Jews in the days of Yehoshua). Others assert that wherever Jews kept two days in the time of the Sanhedrin, they should do so today, even in Eretz Yisrael. Most *poskim* follow the first view. Therefore, we must delineate the borders of Eretz Yisrael.

Eretz Yisrael and Chutz LaAretz

1. Any area in Eretz Yisrael that was conquered either by the Jews who left Egypt or by those who returned after the Babylonian exile[1] observes one day of Yom Tov,[2] even if it is far from Yerushalayim.[3] All other places observe two days of Yom Tov, even if the messengers of the Sanhedrin would have reached them.[4]

---

1. Eretz Yisrael is composed of the areas captured in the days of Yehoshua but not reestablished during the second Commonwealth, and those reestablished in the days of Ezra. The conquests of the *olei Mitzrayim* (those who came up from Egypt) are delineated in Bemidbar 34 and Yehoshua 15. The territories of the *olei Bavel* (those who came up from Babylonia) are listed in *Shevi'is* 6:1 and *Challah* 4.

2. According to the Rambam (*Mishneh Torah, Hilchos Kiddush HaChodesh* 5), only the places reached by messenger observe one day of Yom Tov. Yet one day is observed throughout Eretz Yisrael because we presume that the messengers reached every city therein. The Ritva (*Rosh HaShanah* 18a), however, explains that the enactment of Yom Tov Sheini applies only to Chutz LaAretz, not to Eretz Yisrael— regardless of where the messengers reached. For a full discussion, see *Ir HaKodesh VeHaMikdash*, vol. 3, chap. 19; *Chazon Ish, Orach Chaim*, no. 132; *Tzitz HaKodesh*, vol. 1, no. 42; and *Tzitz Eliezer*, vol. 3, no. 23; and the Hebrew edition of this book, pp. 279-285.

HaGaon Rav Shlomo Zalman Auerbach has told me that perhaps places captured by the *olei Mitzrayim* but not the *olei Bavel* observe one day of Yom Tov, even though they were deserted during the Second Commonwealth. He cites the Rambam (*Mishneh Torah, Hilchos Sanhedrin* 4:6), who rules that *semichah* (appointment to a *beis din* that judges capital crimes) is given within the boundaries of Eretz Yisrael determined by the *olei Mitzrayim*—it is not limited to the areas reestablished by the *olei Bavel*, as is the case for *terumah*, *maaser*, and other laws. The Radvaz adds that the mitzvah of settling in Eretz Yisrael and the privilege of being buried there are also fulfilled in areas conquered by the *olei Mitzrayim*. Therefore, when Chazal restricted Yom Tov Sheini to Chutz LaAretz, as explained by the Ritva, they presumably intended only those areas with no sanctity at all. HaGaon Rav Yosef Shalom Eliashiv concurs.

3. Ritva, *Rosh HaShanah* 18a and *Sukkah* 43a. See note 2.

4. Most contemporary *poskim* accept the Ritva's view.

The East Bank of the Jordan and the Negev

2. The east bank of the Jordan River[5] and all populated parts of the Negev observe one day of Yom Tov.[6]

Gaza

3. The city of Gaza observes one day of Yom Tov.[7]

Eilat

4. Some authorities rule that Jews who live in and around Eilat observe one day of Yom Tov,[8] but others consider this area Chutz LaAretz.[9] Some maintain that residents of Eilat should follow the stringencies of both views.[10]

---

5. The Mishnah (*Shevi'is* 9:2) deems the east bank of the Jordan part of Eretz Yisrael. Also see *Ohr HaChaim* on Bemidbar 32:7 and Devarim 3:13; *Chazon Yechezkel* on *Tosefta, Bava Kamma* 8; *Ir HaKodesh VeHaMikdash*, vol. 3, 19:5; and *Minchas Yitzchak*, vol. 6, no. 127.

6. *Ir HaKodesh VeHaMikdash*, vol. 3, 19:6, in the name of the Chazon Ish; and HaGaon Rav Tzvi Pesach Frank, *Mikraei Kodesh*, Pesach, vol. 2, no. 58.

7. *Kaf HaChaim, Orach Chaim* 496:6, citing *Divrei Yosef*.

8. *Ir HaKodesh VeHaMikdash*, vol. 3, 19:5-6, based on the Ritva. The author cites *Tevuos HaAretz* (in the name of Rav Saadiah Gaon), which equates "Maaleh Akrabim" (Bemidbar 34:4) with Akaba. Hence, the boundaries of the *olei Mitzrayim* extended to Eilat. Also see *Mikraei Kodesh*, Pesach, vol. 2, no. 52:2; and *Tzitz Eliezer*, vol. 3, no. 234.

9. *Shaarei Yitzchak* (12:7, in the name of *Sefer HaMaaser VeHaTerumah*, chap. 5, p. 43) explains that modern-day Eilat is not the same Eilat mentioned in Tanach. Rejecting the arguments of the authorities cited in note 8, the author rules that Jews in Eilat should observe two days. Also see *Mishnas Yosef*, vol. 2, p. 113, and HaGaon Rav Moshe Sternbuch, *Haggadah Shel Pesach*, p. 137. Rav Sternbuch maintains that Eilat has no sanctity whatsoever, and one who lives there is not living in Eretz Yisrael.

10. HaGaon Rav Yosef Shalom Eliashiv and HaGaon Rav Shlomo Zalman Auerbach maintain this position, since we are not sure whether present-day Eilat is indeed within the borders conquered by the *olei Mitzrayim*. See chapter 3, note 4, for the exact procedure.

The Northern Part of Eretz Yisrael

5. The entire northern part of Eretz Yisrael, extending to Tyre and Sidon in present-day Lebanon, remains part of Eretz Yisrael with respect to Yom Tov Sheini.[11]

---

11. *Ir HaKodesh VeHaMikdash* 19:4, in the name of HaGaon Rav Shmuel Salant. But see Rambam, *Pe'er HaDor*, no. 106.

APPENDIX
Local Customs

Introduction

Having clarified the traveler's status vis-à-vis Yom Tov Sheini, we will now examine his relationship to local custom. Chazal say, "One should never depart from [local] custom, lest he create controversy" (*Pesachim* 51a). In this age of travel, many questions arise as to when one must indeed follow local customs contrary to his own. Below are the views of major contemporary *poskim*.

Visiting

1.   When visiting a community whose custom is either more or less stringent than one's own, one may follow his personal practice discreetly,[1] without creating controversy.[2] However, if his custom is

---

1. *Shulchan Aruch* 468:4 and *Mishnah Berurah* ad loc. Also see *Pri Chadash* 468:3; *Minchas Yitzchak*, vol. 4, nos. 1-4; and *Shaarei Yitzchak, Hilchos Yom Tov* 1.

2. *Shulchan Aruch* 468:4. *Chochmas Shlomo* (496:1) forbids any such deviation, even in the presence of one person. However, *BeTzeil HaChochmah* (vol. 1, no. 22:6) notes that others limit this prohibition to acts done in the presence of three or ten. The author concludes that one may ask a local rabbi which view to follow, even though the rabbi will then know that he has a different custom. Also see chapter 6, note 25.

based on an actual point of Jewish law, even a rabbinic one, he may practice it even in public.[3]

2. The first half of the above ruling applies only to customs that are not readily observable, such as waiting three hours between meat and milk in a place where everyone waits six. But obvious departures from the norm, such as performing *melachah* on the afternoon before Pesach,[4] are forbidden even in private.

3. If a visitor is seen observing a variant custom, even in private, he must forgo it, lest he generate controversy. But if he is seen by a Torah scholar, who understands differences in custom, he need not conform.[5]

4. A ben Eretz Yisrael visiting Chutz LaAretz should inconspicuously omit *"Yiru Eineinu"* before the *maariv Shemoneh Esrei.*[6] Conversely, a ben Chutz LaAretz visiting Eretz Yisrael should quietly insert it.[7] In both cases, if this cannot be done discreetly—e.g., if the visitor is serving as the *sheliach tzibbur*—he should follow the local practice.[8]

---

3. *Mishnah Berurah* 468:23.

4. *Mishnah Berurah* 468:14, 23. On *erev Pesach*, some communities refrain from any *melachah* forbidden on Chol HaMoed. Tosafos (*Pesachim* 52a, s.v. *"BeYishuv"*) explains that it is impossible to perform *melachah* discreetly. See *Teshuvos Maharam Alashkar*, no. 49.

5. *Mishnah Berurah* 468:24. The author concludes, however, that it is preferable not to begin following one's personal custom if he knows a Torah scholar is watching him.

6. *Iggeros Moshe, Orach Chaim*, vol. 2, no. 102, and *Yoreh Deah*, vol. 3, no. 96:5.

7. Ibid., *Orach Chaim*, vol. 2, no. 102. *Teshuvah MeAhavah* (vol. 1, no. 91) testifies that the Noda BeYehudah recited *Hallel* on the first night of Pesach even though his congregation did not.

8. *Iggeros Moshe, Orach Chaim*, vol. 2, no. 102. *BeTzeil HaChochmah* (vol. 1, no. 22) states that such a person should not serve as a *sheliach tzibbur*. Nevertheless, one may recite a blessing that he does not normally say in order to avoid dissent. See Rashbam's commentary on *Pesachim* 106a.

Moving

5. As soon as one moves to a new place, he adopts its customs—whether they are more stringent or more lenient than his.[9] He may not even continue his previous practices outside the city or in private.[10] But if people in that city follow various customs, he should preserve his own.[11]

6. Yerushalayim generally has no established custom, nor do the major American cities.[12] Therefore, one who waits three hours between meat and milk—or eats legumes on Pesach—may continue to do so after moving to these places.[13]

7. If someone accustomed to laying tefillin during Chol HaMoed moves to Eretz Yisrael, he may either abandon this practice—in deference to local custom[14]—or continue it[15] in private, omitting

---

9. *Mishnah Berurah* 468:14 and *Bei'ur Halachah* ad loc., s.v. "*HaHoleich.*" Also see *Iggeros Moshe, Orach Chaim,* vol. 1, no. 158.

10. *Mishnah Berurah* 468:14.

11. *Pri Chadash* 468.

12. HaGaon Rav Shlomo Zalman Auerbach explains that Jews move to Yerushalayim from all over the world, each retaining his own customs. (But Eretz Yisrael does have certain practices; see paragraph 7.) HaGaon Rav Moshe Feinstein writes in a similar vein in *Iggeros Moshe* (*Even HaEzer,* vol. 1, no. 59) concerning the United States. He also clarifies why the existence of different customs in one community does not violate the biblical injunction of *lo sisgodedu* (do not form factions in Torah observance). See the Hebrew edition of this book, *Miluim,* section 2.

13. This is based on a ruling by HaGaon Rav Shlomo Zalman Auerbach.

14. *Iggeros Moshe, Orach Chaim,* vol. 4, no. 105;5. Although laying tefillin is a Torah obligation, one may be lenient, as were the Jews who founded the present-day community in Eretz Yisrael and established its customs. See *Pesachim* 51a and *Chullin* 18a regarding one's obligation to adopt even lenient local customs.

15. *Iggeros Moshe, Orach Chaim,* vol. 4, no. 105:5. Since today some people do lay tefillin on Chol HaMoed, not doing so may no longer be the custom of Eretz Yisrael. Moreover, among the authorities who see no mitzvah in laying tefillin on Chol HaMoed, some do not forbid it. HaGaon Rav Shlomo Zalman Auerbach and HaGaon Rav Chaim Pinchus Scheinberg concur with this ruling. HaGaon Rav Auerbach adds that, according to some authorities, refraining from laying tefillin constitutes a violation of the Torah, so he may continue his practice in Eretz Yisrael.

the blessing.[16] In the latter case, he should mentally stipulate that if he is obligated to wear tefillin, he is doing so for the sake of the mitzvah, and if not, he is wearing them as a regular garment.[17]

Prayer

8. One should adopt the local *nusach*, even when reciting the silent *Shemoneh Esrei*. Therefore, if someone accustomed to saying *"Shalom Rav"* in *minchah* on Shabbos moves to Eretz Yisrael, he should recite *"Sim Shalom"* instead. Likewise, a ben Chutz LaAretz who moves to Eretz Yisrael should recite *"Ein Kelokeinu"* after *shacharis*.[18]

9. When davening with a congregation that follows *nusach Sephard*, one should adopt this *nusach* for *pesukei dezimrah* and the blessings before and after the Shema. If this is difficult for him, he may

---

16. *Iggeros Moshe, Orach Chaim*, vol. 4, no. 105:5. Since there may be no mitzvah to lay tefillin on Chol HaMoed, those who do should omit the blessing.

According to *Beis Yitzchak* (*Yoreh Deah*, vol. 2, no. 88), better one should daven alone on Chol HaMoed than with ten men who aren't wearing tefillin. For in the latter case, one can lay tefillin privately and repeat the Shema, but not the blessings beforehand and afterward. Yet the Mishnah Berurah (46:32) and HaGaon Rav Shlomo Zalman Auerbach (see chapter 4, note 24) prefer that one daven with a minyan.

Although *Beis Yitzchak* indicates that one should not wear tefillin unless the congregation does, the Maharsham (vol. 3, no. 359) maintains that since we may be obligated to wear them, one who does so does not transgress *lo sisgodedu* even if no one else in the congregation follows suit.

17. This is based on a ruling by HaGaon Rav Shlomo Zalman Auerbach. The Mishnah Berurah (31:8) rules that one should make such a stipulation even in a place where it is customary to wear tefillin on Chol HaMoed.

18. This is the ruling of HaGaon Rav Shlomo Zalman Auerbach, based on *Pesachim* 51a. "*Sim Shalom*" is recited during *minchah* on Shabbos because it refers to the "*Toras chaim*," which one has just read (Rema, *Orach Chaim* 127:2). Since this is the custom in all of Eretz Yisrael, one must adopt it when moving there, unlike the situation described in note 12.

See *BeTzeil HaChochmah*, vol. 4, no. 121, concerning *Yizkor* customs.

quietly follow *nusach Ashkenaz*.[19] In any case, he should recite the *Shemoneh Esrei* in accordance with his own custom,[20] and *Kedushah* in accordance with the congregation's even if he says it quietly.[21] If he serves as the *sheliach tzibbur*, some authorities rule that he should recite the silent *Shemoneh Esrei* in accordance with his custom and the repetition in acordance with the congregation's,[22] while others maintain that he should recite the silent *Shemoneh Esrei* in accordance with the congregation as well.[23]

10. One should recite *Viduy* and the Thirteen Attributes of Divine Mercy before *Tachanun* if the congregation follows this custom.[24] If one customarily recites these prayers but the congregation does not, he should recite *Viduy* inconspicuously (without striking his chest) but omit the Thirteen Attributes.[25]

11. A Sephardic Jew may not adopt the *nusach* or enunciation of Ashkenazic Jewry, nor may an Ashkenazic Jew adapt himself to

---

19. *Iggeros Moshe, Orach Chaim*, vol. 2, no. 23. Nonetheless, following the congregation's custom is preferable to trying to remember to recite these prayers quietly, since they are usually said aloud.

20. *Iggeros Moshe, Orach Chaim*, vol. 2, no. 23; *Sho'eil U'Meishiv, Mahadurah* 3, no. 247; *Meishiv Davar*, no. 17; and *Minchas Yitzchak*, vol. 7, no. 5. *Pe'as HaShulchan* (no. 3) rules that one must follow the *nusach* of the congregation, but HaGaon Rav Shlomo Zalman Auerbach reports that this is not customary.

21. *Meishiv Davar*, no. 17; *Iggeros Moshe, Orach Chaim*, vol. 2, no. 23; and *Minchas Yitzchak*, vol. 7, no. 5. Defying the congregation here would be akin to reciting *Kedushah* privately, which is forbidden. Also see R. Akiva Eiger's glosses on *Orach Chaim* 128, in the name of *Kisvei HaAri*.

22. *Sho'eil U'Meishiv, Mahadurah* 3, no. 247. See chapter 11, paragraph 6.

23. *Iggeros Moshe, Orach Chaim*, vol. 2, no. 29. The *sheliach tzibbur* recites the silent *Shemoneh Esrei* in order to become familiar with the *Shemoneh Esrei* he will recite aloud. Therefore, he should recite the same *nusach* he will be reciting during the repetition.

With regard to altering one's *nusach*, *Iggeros Moshe* does not distinguish between Sephardic and Chassidic congregations.

24. *Iggeros Moshe, Orach Chaim*, vol. 3, no. 89.

25. Ibid., vol. 4, no. 34.

Sephardic custom.[26] But if, for example, an Ashkenazic Jew settles in a Sephardic community located in an Arab country, he should adopt the Sephardic practice.[27]

12. If a Sephardic Jew studies in an Ashkenazic yeshiva (or vice versa), most contemporary authorities rule that he may not alter his custom.[28] But some disagree.[29] Nevertheless, children of Chassidic parents may adopt *nusach Ashkenaz*.[30]

13. A school serving both Ashkenazim and Sephardim should follow the *nusach* and enunciation of the majority of its students.[31]

14. If an Ashkenazic synagogue has come to serve more Sephardim than Ashkenazim but the latter constitute a substantial minority, it should remain Ashkenazic. Thus, it should not make changes in keeping with Sephardic custom, like reciting *Hoshanos* after *mussaf* instead of beforehand. Yet it may introduce new prayers— such as "*Mizmor LeDavid*" on the nights of Rosh HaShanah and Yom Kippur, or "*Shir HaMaalos*" after "*Yishtabach*" during the Ten Days of Repentance, or *Hallel* on the first night of Pesach—provided that most of the congregation consents.[32]

---

26. Ibid., vol. 1, no. 68. Concerning enunciation, see vol. 3, no. 5, and *Minchas Yitzchak*, vol. 3, no. 9.

27. *Iggeros Moshe*, vol. 3, no. 5, and vol. 4, no. 33.

28. HaGaon Rav Y. Y. Kanievsky, *Karyana DeAggarsa*, no. 138:3. Yet the prohibition against deviating from one's custom may be waived for the sake of one's Torah education. For example, Ashkenazic parents may send their child to a school that teaches Sephardic enunciation if the only alternative is a less religious school. HaGaon Rav Shlomo Zalman Auerbach is also lenient in certain cases of peer pressure. In such situations, a halachic authority should be consulted.

29. In *Eidus LeYisrael* (p. 162), HaGaon Rav Yosef Eliyahu Henkin writes: "If an Ashkenazic Jew always prays in a Sephardic synagogue, he may adopt the custom of the congregation."

30. *Iggeros Moshe, Orach Chaim*, vol. 2, no. 24. Since the early Chassidim abandoned *nusach Ashkenaz* for *nusach Sephard*, a member of that community may revert to the original custom.

31. HaGaon Rav Y. Y. Kanievsky, *Karyana DeAggarsa*, no. 138:4.

32. *Iggeros Moshe, Orach Chaim*, vol. 2, no. 51.

Establishing a New Community

15. A new community must adopt the customs of the majority of its members, even if this majority eventually becomes the minority.[33] If there is no majority custom, the community may adopt the practices of any segment of its population.[34]

Fasts

16. If one is out of town when his city commences a one-time public fast, he need not observe it.[35] Yet he must participate in the city's annual fasts (for example, Poles fast on the twentieth of Sivan), no matter where he is when they begin.[36] But if he moves, he need not observe these fasts, even if he happens to be back in the city as they are starting.[37]

If one visits a city on a fast day that is not observed in his community, he must fast for the duration of his visit,[38] even if he already ate that morning.[39] But if he arrives at midday and leaves that afternoon, he may resume eating.[40] In any case, if he is too weak to fast, he may eat privately.[41]

---

33. Ibid., *Yoreh Deah*, vol. 1, no. 81.

34. Ibid., vol. 2, no. 15.

35. *Shulchan Aruch* 574:1 and *Mishnah Berurah* ad loc.

36. *Mishnah Berurah* 574:1, in the name of the Pri Megadim.

37. *Aruch HaShulchan* 574:1 and *Mishnah Berurah* 574:1.

38. *Shulchan Aruch* 574:2. The Magen Avraham adds that although with respect to other customs regarding eating, one may follow his lenient practice in private, here he should ally himself with the congregation in its time of trouble. Consequently, if the fast commemorates a past event, it would seem permissible for the visitor to eat in private. But *Mishnah Berurah* (574:3) notes that the Eliyah Rabbah is stringent even in this case.

39. *Mishnah Berurah* 574:2.

40. *Shulchan Aruch* 574:2.

41. *Shaar HaTziyun* 574:4, in the name of the Pri Megadim.

A Woman's Customs after Marriage

17. A wife adopts her husband's customs, even if they are more lenient or stringent than her own,[42] which she need not formally annul.[43] Therefore, a Sephardic woman who marries an Ashkenazic man follows Ashkenazic customs and an Ashkenazic woman who marries a Sephardic man adopts Sephardic practices.[44] Some authorities rule that a husband may allow his wife to maintain her own customs.[45]

18. If a husband's family does not allow its women to wear wigs while his wife's family does, she must follow the local custom.[46]

19. If a wife moves to a place where married women leave a little of their hair uncovered, she may do the same, even if she comes from a more stringent community.[47] Likewise, if she lives among married women who cover their hair completely, she must follow suit, regardless of what she's used to.[48]

---

42. *Iggeros Moshe, Orach Chaim,* vol. 1, no. 158. HaGaon Rav Shlomo Zalman Auerbach states that a woman's status changes under the *chuppah,* even before she enters her husband's home. I have also heard this ruling from HaGaon Rav Yehudah Tzadkah. But *Minchas Yitzchak* insists that she only begins following her husband's customs when she moves into his home.

43. *Iggeros Moshe, Orach Chaim,* vol. 1, no. 158. HaGaon Rav Shlomo Zalman Auerbach explains that since a woman adopts her husband's customs, she is only bound by her father's until her wedding.

44. *Iggeros Moshe, Even HaEzer,* vol. 1, no. 59.

45. This is based on a ruling by HaGaon Rav Shlomo Zalman Auerbach. A wife adopts her husband's customs because of her marital obligations towards him. Therefore, the husband may waive these obligations. For instance, husbands commonly allow their wives to retain their *nusach.* If a wife adopts her husband's custom but he later allows her to resume her own, she must annul the custom she has observed since marriage. Similarly, if she continues her custom after marriage but later wishes to adopt her husband's, she must annul her former practice.

46. *Iggeros Moshe, Even HaEzer,* vol. 2, no. 12, and vol. 4, no. 100:4. If a husband's practices defy local norms, his wife need not follow them. Also see *Iggeros Moshe, Yoreh Deah,* vol. 1, no. 81.

47. *Bei'ur Halachah* 75, s.v. "MiChutz," in the name of the Magen Avraham.

48. Ibid. Also see *Iggeres Moshe, Even HaEzer,* vol. 1, no. 59.

INDEX

Dedicated in loving honor
to my parents,
Andrew and Myra Fried שיח׳
of Indianapolis,
and my mother-in-law,
Mrs. Sarah Morgenstern תחי׳
of Bayit Vegan.
May they live long, happy, and healthy lives,
and derive much *nachas* from
their children and grandchildren.

אלה יעמדו על הברכה
בהצלחה וכל טוב בכל מעשיך

ר׳ חיים יונה קופל נ״י ורעי׳ תח׳
בית וגן־ניו יורק
ר׳ ישראל קמחי נ״י ורע׳ תח׳
בית וגן